POETIC VOYAGES COVENTRY

Edited by Heather Killingray

First published in Great Britain in 2001 by
YOUNG WRITERS
Remus House,
Coltsfoot Drive,
Peterborough, PE2 9JX
Telephone (01733) 890066

HB ISBN 0 75432 590 3
SB ISBN 0 75432 591 1

FOREWORD

Young Writers was established in 1991 with the aim to promote creative writing in children, to make reading and writing poetry fun.

This year once again, proved to be a tremendous success with over 88,000 entries received nationwide.

The Poetic Voyages competition has shown us the high standard of work and effort that children are capable of today. It is a reflection of the teaching skills in schools, the enthusiasm and creativity they have injected into their pupils shines clearly within this anthology.

The task of selecting poems was therefore a difficult one but nevertheless, an enjoyable experience. We hope you are as pleased with the final selection in *Poetic Voyages Coventry* as we are.

CONTENTS

Alex Allen	58
Joe McCauley	58
Usman Khan	59
Colin McCann	59
Laura Tipple	59
Emily Honey	60
Penny Woolley	60
Danielle Noble	61
Tarnjit Kaur Bhambra	61
Francesca Kirtley-Paine	62
Andrew Bowell	62
Hannah Kirtley-Paine	63
Kieran Orchard	63
Shona Hands	64
Lauren Smee	64
Jade Kelly	65
Natasha Jackson	65
Mitchell Bailey	66
Aaron Allen	66
Trisha Prajapati	66
Michelle McLean	67
Dean Barlow	67
Hayden Ludford	68
Mark Coyles	68
Sonia Gherra	69
Kieran Merrick	69
Tasmin Mills	70
Nicolette Bazeley	70

Joseph Cash Primary School
Zirah Khan	70
Jonathan Bentley	71
Jordan Arrol	72
Jack Downing	72

Limbrick Wood Primary School
Elisha Henry	72
Jamie Elliott	73

Amy Andrews	91
Jusreen Sangha	91
Emily Flynn	92
Amani Bone	92
James Brown	93
Rachel Franklin	93
Anna Johnston	94
Ashleigh Davies	94
Connor McGrath	95
Georgina Oag	95
Chanice Mancini	96
Emily Sherwood	96
Edward Kimberley	97
James Askew	97
Jake Spencer	98
Stephanie Lambell	98
Vincent Marzetti-Cook	99
Louise Faulkner	99
Lauren Tighe	99
Francesca Rigby	100
Marie Low	100
Bethan Schofield	101
Dale Brogan	102
Catherine Frankton	103

Moseley Primary School

Daniella Da Silva	103
Alison Hagyard	104
Mark Taylor	104
Robert West	105
Sophie Reddington	105
Jennifer Bowers	106
Victoria Heggie	107
Kieran Cunningham	108
Emily Gill	109
Neelam Patel	109
Junaid Duberia	110
Samantha Pepper	110

The Poems

THE ONE AND ONLY FLOWER

When the broken wind fails to blow
When the nature in the world goes way too slow
The fields are empty, all that's living is smashed,
Except that one and only flower that managed to last

When the sun gives light but not enough
When life seems to end up way too tough
When life has given up and drifted away
The one and only flower feels it should stay.

When the world instead of spinning, bends
When all happiness seems to end
When everything feels it shouldn't be alive,
The one and only flower is determined to survive.

When all the water washes away,
When the sun falls further day by day
When all the other flowers just want to die
The one and only flower prays to the sky.

When all of our nature begins to fall down
When everyone's head spins round and round
When the one and only flower tells them life can be cured
All the world is reassured.

Kate Vine (10)
Balsall Common Primary School

THE LAND OF THE MIDNIGHT SUN

Caribou gallop across the shore,
A shore of not sand but snow,
Ice cracks beneath delicate feet,
Feet galloping - unaware of where to go

Wind is howling,
A blizzard breaks,
Under grey-white skies,
Seals dive into frosty water,
Before their very eyes

Hoof prints lie forgotten,
Hidden in the cloudy mist,
Suddenly wind scoops them up,
They are not to be missed.

In the Land of the Midnight Sun.

Amy Baker (9)
Balsall Common Primary School

TOY HEAVEN

Books here
Games there
Paper scattered
Everywhere
Hama beads
Plastic sword
I don't think I'll ever
Ever get bored.

PlayStation 2
And a Dreamcast,
Playing games,
Ever so fast
Big cuddly toys
Having fun
I'll never leave . . .
Toy heaven!

Emily Garrett (9)
Balsall Common Primary School

DRAGON

A dragon has green slimy skin
And a really fiery tongue
It wraps itself up nice and warm
And counts sheep to fall asleep

In the morning it wakes up hungry
Wondering what to eat
Its mouth starts to water
Thinking of the sheep

He loves sheep for his breakfast
It's the best you can ever have!
He goes straight into the field
And herds up all the sheep

He breathes out fast and starts a fire
Then finds a cooking pot
He starts to think of tasty lamb
Then wakes up like a shot

Rebecca Deeley (8)
Balsall Common Primary School

THE TIME OF MY LIFE

In Florida I wish to be,
Where there is a light blue sea,
There is Blizzard Beach
And if you get some time to reach,
Magic Kingdom, is just for you
And you can meet Winnie the Pooh.
Tigger, Piglet and Mickey Mouse
And you can go in Minnie's house
As for Epcot, as you can see.
Is made for the future for you and me
Pleasure Island is a trance,
Where you can sing, party or dance.
If you want to see some wildlife,
Go to the Animal Kingdom and have a ride,
On the safari truck
Where you go in lots of muck.
All these and more are in Disneyland
And I'll give you a hand.
Go to this special place,
And a smile will always be on your face.

Sarah Brown (10)
Balsall Common Primary School

NATURE IN HARMONY

Imagine the waves splashing on the bay
Imagine the fish playing with me,
We looked out of our sailing boat
And what we saw was nature in harmony.

Imagine the rabbits burrow low and deep
Imagine the birds high up in the tree,
We looked out of our cottage window
And what we saw was nature in harmony.

Imagine the chimneys blowing out smoke
Imagine pollution how bad can it be,
We looked out from our house
And we said don't spoil nature in harmony.

Lydia Sharples (8)
Balsall Common Primary School

CHRISTMAS CAROLS

C   andy to hang on the Christmas tree
H   anging baubles there will be
R   acing through the snow
I   sing Christmas carols I know
S   ilently sleeping through the night
T   his is my candle for my light
M   y presents hang below the tree
A   nd thinking what Santa brings
S   anta is coming tonight.

C   old winter nights
A   ll people singing
R   olling through the snow
O   h! Singing.
L   ovely carols
S   inging at the sky!

Beth Hancock (8)
Balsall Common Primary School

A Pirate's Life

A pirate's life is a life for me,
Yo! Ho! Ho! and a bottle of rum.
I get seasick on the sea,
Yo! Ho! Ho! and a bottle of rum.
Hoist the sails way up high,
Yo! Ho! Ho! and a bottle of rum.
Near the crow's nest in the sky,
Yo! Ho! Ho! and a bottle of rum.
Bound for an island way out west.
Yo! Ho! Ho! and a bottle of rum.
This will be a proper quest,
Yo! Ho! Ho! and a bottle of rum.
There we'll find a treasure chest,
Yo! Ho! Ho! and a bottle of rum.

Emma Fairbrother (9)
Balsall Common Primary School

Pirates

A pirates' ship has a crow's nest
But there are lots of little pests
The captain wears a big black patch

He also wears a hat to match
They hoist the sails hoist the sails
On the ship there are lots of males
Some pirates wear an earring
But they're not very caring
Pirates drink lots of beer
Which makes them unsteady and unable to steer
A pirates' flag flies very high
As the ship passes by.

Katrina Maxwell (9)
Balsall Common Primary School

SLEEPY, SLEEPY

Sleepy, sleepy,
Tired in my bed
I want to snuggle up now
So where is my Ted

Catherine West (8)
Balsall Common Primary School

A BUMBLE BEE

A people stinger
A honey bringer
        A fluffy flyer
        A slow die-er
A wall sticker
A pollen licker
        Buzzz!

Stefan Jardim (10)
Bournebrook CE Primary School

BILLY BASS

I am fat, slimy, wet and cold
But I am fat and bold.
I weigh two pounds
I hate the ground.
I have got a flipper tail the size of a mat
You cannot pat me on the back.

Jake Mason (10)
Bournebrook CE Primary School

THE SEA

I am the one who keeps the world together
I will be here for ever and ever
I have been around for years and years
I am strong and brave, I have no fears.

When I am angry I roar and roar
And roar and roar some more.
I flood your beautiful seaside homes
When I will strike no one knows.

When I am happy I lay calm and quiet,
I really don't think it's time for a riot.
As I lie without a sound,
I watch the world go round and round.

Emily Dodd (11)
Bournebrook CE Primary School

MY SISTER

A loud squawker
A big talker

An annoying thing
A bee sting

A lousy fighter
A good biter

All to make my sister.

Natalie Rowlands (11)
Bournebrook CE Primary School

Too Old To Work

I can wait patiently as the lorries pass by
Along my great steel back I roar a great sigh!

I count the passing traffic
One, two, three four,
I have heard my family rumbling
Crashing to the floor.

I am centuries old, heavy, big and bold,
I have lived through the ages, warm
Hot and cold.

But now I have come to my end
I say goodbye, goodbye to you all.

Lorna Crowley (10)
Bournebrook CE Primary School

Puppy

A fuzzy ball of fun
A bouncy run

A wet sticky nose
A tail that grows

A woofer on legs
An animal that begs

A cat fighter
A slipper biter

A bone lover
A person shover

Stacey Hammond (10)
Bournebrook CE Primary School

TORNADO

I can whip through houses
or anything I see.
Blow down trees,
travel through water with ease.

If you get in my way, I won't
stop or wait.
Don't even think I'll hesitate.

I'll get faster, and faster,
whizzing everywhere.
You're so lucky, oh so lucky, to escape
when I'm there.

If you have brains, you'll
surely see,
I have no heart or feelings
in me.

Sophie Taylor (10)
Bournebrook CE Primary School

THE TORTOISE

I hide in a shell at night,
and when I do I get a fright.

When my friend comes around
I say hello, and hang around.

When it's night I say goodnight,
I will see you tomorrow, in the sunlight.

Rowan Taylor (10)
Bournebrook CE Primary School

THE SNOW

I can cover the ground with a
white carpet of snow
reach all things high and low.

I can land everywhere on
the ground
Without making the
slightest sound.

I can make things freeze for
I am cruel and cold,
You have to wrap up warm
because you've been told

I can land in snowflakes and
different shapes
Freeze all dirty horrible lakes.

Niamh Luckett (11)
Bournebrook CE Primary School

THERE WAS A VERY THICK BAT

There was a very thick bat
Who stupidly fell on a mat,
When along came a dog
Who threw him in a bog
And then came out as a cat.

Phillip Grove (10)
Bournebrook CE Primary School

KITTEN

A soft ball
A quick listen to a call

     A long tail
     A faint wail

          A gently lick
          A fast catcher of a stick

     A cute roll
     An eater from a bowl

For I am a purrrrfect
Kitten.

Kerrie McCloy (10)
Bournebrook CE Primary School

THE SUN

I can burn the people of the world,
and scorch all the gardens curled.

I can make people happy I can make people sad
but they soon forget that because all the fun they had.

I can shine through your windows and give you light
and I go behind clouds for the night.

I can annoy children in the school,
and other people think I'm cool.

Amy Metcalf (10)
Bournebrook CE Primary School

THERE WAS A YOUNG GIRL FROM JUPITER

There was a young girl from Jupiter
Who just couldn't get any stupider
She flew away
On the coldest day
That happened to the girl from Jupiter.

Marian Towell (10)
Bournebrook CE Primary School

FEAR

I am what people think up in their minds
And I love to tease people that are kind.

I'll send a spine-tingling chill down your back
And you'll hate it if you hear it crack.

Luke Garratley (11)
Bournebrook CE Primary School

WINTER

Have you seen the snow fluttering all around?
Have you seen it landing on the ground?
Have you see the snowmen standing all around?
The snow is falling from the sky and I don't know why.
I saw the snow in the night and it's a lovely sight.

Kamran Bal (8)
Cannon Park Primary School

BULLIES

'Oy Chris! I mean you!
You look like a turtle on the loo.
You're fat, not thin, dumb and small,
You ain't got guts like me at all.'

Chris ran home to tell his mummy
His mother said 'Don't worry honey,
I'll look after you, you little bunny.'
But Chris did not find that too funny.

The kids are horrid and mess about,
But the teachers are worse when they shout.
They're nasty and ugly and bigger than me,
Can't wait 'til it's hometime at half-past three.

His nose was runny, his eyes were red.
'I'm not going to school,' he said.
'I'm just going to stay in bed.
But you can't do that . . . you're the *Head!*'

Nathan Wilson (9)
Cannon Park Primary School

NOISES

Listen with your ears
What can you hear?
I can hear a bee
Buzzing merrily.
I can hear a growl
Giving me a scowl.
I can hear a clang
Then another bang!

Calvin Chen (8)
Cannon Park Primary School

RISKS

Plugs and sockets they
overload
I'm just surprised they
don't explode,
Wires twisting
everywhere,
Just like crazy
curly hair,
Don't put your
fingers in there
You'll get a surprise,
so will your parents
when they see your
grilled disguise.
You could die from
shocking electricity,
You'll end up down
Casualty,
You'll be left with
scars forever,
So don't play near
electricity *ever.*

Cally Healy (10)
Cannon Park Primary School

SNOW

Look out the window
What do you see?
I see the snow looking at me
Look at the snowflakes in the sky
Look at the one that catches your eye.

Lahna Patel (7)
Cannon Park Primary School

SNOW

Look out the window, you can see a tree and snow.
Now you can play at snowballs and make a snowman.
Look out of the window
Tell me what you see?
There's white snow, quite like light.

Shuhei Kato (8)
Cannon Park Primary School

SNOW

Look out of the window
What do you see?
I see a snowflake falling onto a tree
The snow is very, very white
When I went outside
I saw the snowflakes falling onto me.

Bethany Austin (7)
Cannon Park Primary School

THE SNOW

The ground is white
The snow is light
And I had a fright!
Oh, what fun to have a run
In the snow.

Gil Sinclair Julio (8)
Cannon Park Primary School

THE SECRETS THAT ONLY I KNOW

I'm about to tell you a secret,
Don't tell anyone, please, please.
The secret is very secretive, you know
So don't tell a soul
No! Not even a friend.
The secret is very funny, you will think,
But actually it's quite nice to hear.

Funny the secret is, but you can keep it, I know.
And the secret is about a creature, gentle,
And its wings are as soft as snow.
I think one day I'll see the secret spring or jump in front of my eyes.
Really, I think it will, I'm not telling lies.
You believe in this secret, so do, really, yes do, please.

Sally Taylor (9)
Cannon Park Primary School

SNOW

Look out the window
What do you see?
I see some people make a snowman
I see my friends having a snowball fight.
Look out the window
What do you see?
I see some snow looking at me.
I see some bright snow and
I see a snowman looking at me.

Keyleigh Jassi-Marston (7)
Cannon Park Primary School

SNOW

Look out of the window
What can you see?
Snowflakes floating down to say
Build a snowman for me.
Snowballs are fun
Snow onto me.
Snowballs are fun.
Look out of the window
What can you see?
A white tree
You can see some snow melting.

Jennifer Higgerson (7)
Cannon Park Primary School

SNOW

Look out of the window,
What can you see?
I can see the white snowflake
Staring at me.
Look out of the window
What can you see?
I can see a child building a snowman.
Look out of the window
What can you see?
I can see a rabbit playing in the snow
And it is about to go.

Penny Matthews (8)
Cannon Park Primary School

SNOWFLAKES AT MY WINDOW

The snowflakes at my window
Look through the window
What do you see
A white piece of snow staring at me

Look through the window
What do you see?
A white snowy tree scaring me.

Look through the window
What do you see
Five little bees as cold as me.

Naomi Kirkwood (8)
Cannon Park Primary School

SNOWING OUTSIDE

Looking out the window
What do you see?
I see a snowflake falling onto a tree
Look of the window, what can you hear?
I can hear a buzzing noise just like a bee.
Look out the window
What do you feel?
I feel something very cold
Up to my knees.

Jason Hseu (7)
Cannon Park Primary School

THE ANGEL'S SONG

Give peace to everyone, everybody here
Even those who hide away, those who live in fear.
Even though we can't help him, who hides away
Let him summon all his strength and find the peace that was
                                           meant to be

In our journey, help us see
That everybody he or she
Will live forever in harmony
Let them see the peace and love
Let them reach to the stars above
All we need now is a love that's constant and won't let go.

Rosemary Jones (9)
Cannon Park Primary School

LOOKING OUT OF THE WINDOW

Look out of the window
Tell me what you see?
I see snowflakes spinning merrily!
Look out of the window,
Tell me what you see?
I see a tree singing, just like me!
Look out of the window,
Tell me what you see?
I see a robin, flying straight at me.

Sami Baba (7)
Cannon Park Primary School

CHRISTMAS

C rackers opened and killer toys revealed
H erod murdered baby boys and their life was sealed.
R udolph delivers bombs to every child that lives
I n the night Santa comes with a curse to give
S anta crept in and stole out a knife
T atters, the curtains were in, so was my life.
M urderous Santa is a killer
A nd so watch out for Santa's murderous caterpillar
S o in all Santa's dead, blood spurts out from his cracked head.

Katherine Jane Raison (9) & Emma Louise Sawyer (10)
Cannon Park Primary School

LOOKING OUT THE WINDOW

Looking out the window, what do I see?
I see a Christmas tree waving to me, waving to me.
Looking out the window, what do I hear?
I hear a car without a gear, without a gear.
Looking out the window, what can I smell?
I can smell some roses growing by the well,
Growing by the well.

Vanya Rumynin (7)
Cannon Park Primary School

WINTER DAYS

I think winter is the best,
It is better than the rest.
Winter always brings the snow,
It always makes my fingers glow.
In winter people always play,
They stick and hang around all day.
Yes, I think winter is the best,
It really is better than the rest.

George Dore (9)
Cannon Park Primary School

SPRING

When flowers spring up lightly
When the sun shines brightly
Flowers pop up all around
See the birds bob
See the flowers pop
That's *spring!*

Shamira Naidu-Young (8)
Cannon Park Primary School

SNOW

We can make a snowman
When it snows
We can make a snowball too
When it snows a lot
We shovel the snow
It snows quietly and gently.

Miki Sawabe (7)
Cannon Park Primary School

MEMORIES

Summer was such a happy time
Now it is so cold.
Looking forward to summer again
And I've got a cold
Winter is a happy time
The best thing is the snow

We are going to sunny Spain next year
There won't be any snow there.
We will be leaving the rain back here
So enjoy the seasons as they come.
The snow, the sun, whatever the weather.

Faith Hannon (10)
Cannon Park Primary School

FRIENDSHIP

Friendship is happiness
Love, joy and sadness
Together and forever
Hope and laughter
Joy is the most important
It goes with luck
Upset a few times because you broke up
But then you meet once again
And joy, love and friendship
Are around.

Shakira Rushion (9)
Cannon Park Primary School

MY DOGS

I have a cuddly collie
With the common name of Ben
I also have a lurcher
With the rhyming name of Pen(ny)

I have to walk them every day
Come hail, rain or shine
And when mum says it's time for walkies
You should hear me whine!

When Ben does his begging tricks
He always makes us laugh
But as for Penny, well
She's not quite so smart.

Ben has a problem
Not a very big one at all.
Only his body is rather long
And his legs are rather small.

Penny is a mad lurcher
She runs around all day
When she isn't eating
She's getting in the way!

Whatever they do
Whatever I say
I can't help but love them
In every way!

Lauren Sumner (9)
Cannon Park Primary School

FIREWORKS

F ireworks are pretty and bright
I n the night, cool they rule
R unning kids all around
E very bonfire night
W olves howl
O range, blue, yellow and green
R ocks rumble
K reep, crack
S leep in the snow, fast asleep forever.

Alicia Sheppard (10)
Cannon Park Primary School

SPACE

My spaceship,
travelling through space,
seeing all the bright stars,
looking down at the sea.
Going to planet Mars,
passing by Jupiter,
looking at the stars again.

Getting onto Mars,
looking round at all the planets,
looking down, down at the sea,
standing on planet Mars.

Calling all the spacemen,
looking for help tonight.
The spaceship has broken down,
The spaceship is going again.

Steven Jones (9)
Hearsall Community Primary School

WHEN I WENT TO FIND SANTA CLAUS

When I went to find Santa Claus,
It took a very long time,
I had to go to Lapland
To find dear Santa Claus.

When I went to find Santa Claus,
To give him my letter,
I found him in his bed,
Having a little Christmas rest.

When I went to find Santa Claus,
I found him in Lapland,
So I gave him my letter,
And a big, big hug.

When I went to find Santa Claus,
I wandered round his workshop,
To play with all the other toys,
And then I went home to leave him to rest.

Bridget Roberts (10)
Hearsall Community Primary School

FLYING SKATEBOARD

I was orbiting Earth at ten miles an hour,
In a race of celebrities bigger than Tim Bower.
I did a three sixty that looked like a pixie.
I saw a canary that flew like a fairy.
I did an olly that looked like a dolly,
And then I woke up!

Phillip Child (10)
Hearsall Community Primary School

RAINBOW ANGER

Be quiet and leave me alone.
I hate you, shut up.
I'll never talk to you again.
Go away, slam the door,
Let me do what I like.

Red is my feeling, I feel red.
Red-hot, big, bad, red.
I want to be red,
Red is good for me.
Yes, I like being red.

Pink embarrassed. People laugh at pink.
I hate pink, you are humiliating me pink,
Embarrassing me. I've made a fool of myself.
I hate pink.

Big, black hole in my mind.
Down a hole, black hole, dark, black,
Down low, dark, cold, alone, unfriendly, sad.

Blue thinking, deep blue thinking.
What have I done? Why did I do it?
I shouldn't, I'm sorry.
Blue mood.

Green, I've apologised, I'm sorry.
I'm green, I'm calm, peaceful,
Colour of tranquil.
I'm OK, I'm green.

Emily Bell (11)
Hearsall Community Primary School

TIME MACHINE

What's that? It's a time machine, I'm going in.
It was amazing, yeah!
It was so cool, yeah!

It's the 1930s
It was so old,
You can't buy gold.

It's the 1940s
This is the war,
They're looking really poor.

It's the 1950s
The king died, the queen was crowned,
Mrs Winters was born, the king's father frowned.

It's the 1960s
A scorching rocket set off round about noon,
Neil Armstrong set foot on the moon,

It's the 1970s
Something happened with Apollo 13
Luckily they survived and worked as a team

It's the 1980s
My favourite TV programme was invented
My brother was born but was only a kid.

It's the 1990s
I was born, me, me, me,
But I cut my knee, knee, knee.

It's 2000
Millennium, millennium
Yeah! Yeah!

That was good
What happened? Nothing big.

Jack Matthew Curry (10)
Hearsall Community Primary School

THE VOYAGE OF EVAPORATION

The water is silent
More silent than the moon,
And the sun glows red
Sending waves of burning heat.

Now up I rise
Now I'm transparent,
More clear than a window
Becoming a light cloud.

Floating towards the mountain peak
Feeling very heavy now,
Expanding even more now
This is how the ride starts.

Down, down, down I go
Rapid it is but only a stream,
Faster, faster and faster I go
Heading for the giant blue sea.

The ride has stopped
The rapids have gone,
I flow with the sea
Then I float up again.

Nicholas Edwards (11)
Hearsall Community Primary School

PIRATES

Pirates, pirates
Swords and daggers.
Pirates, pirates
Fighting enemies.
Pirates, pirates
Walk the plank.
Pirates, pirates
Everywhere.
Pirates, pirates
Fire the canons.
Pirates, pirates
Patched-up eyes.
Pirates, pirates
Swords and fists.
Pirates, pirates
Taking over.
Pirates, pirates
Abandon ship.
Pirates, pirates
The battle ends.

Umar Ali Mahmood (10)
Hearsall Community Primary School

MAGNIFICENT SPACE

My bright coloured spaceship,
Whizzing through stars,
From Mars to Venus,
Dodging around,
Shooting stars,
Swiss moon.
Dancing in the moonlight.

Sun rising,
Flames around me.
Going down to Earth,
Now I'm landing.

Sanum Tariq (11)
Hearsall Community Primary School

TRAVELLING ACROSS THE SEA

Travelling across the blue seas,
Rain not in the blue sea,
Along we go on the blue sea.
Voyages across the blue sea, how wonderful!
Enjoy the trip!
Lovely view from the boat.
Landscape of the sea.
In a boat travelling across the blue sea.
No traffic, nothing, it's calm!
Going far away from all those, going in the calm.

Around the world we go!
Coming everywhere on the sea.
Right and left the boat goes
On the big blue ocean.
Seeing the dolphins going up and down.
Seeing the birds flying gently.

The boat moving gently,
High in the sky, seeing the birds going from the boat.
Enjoy, how enjoying!

Sea, how beautiful it is.
Enjoy it very much
Around we went and now we go on the land.

Liina Sobratee (9)
Hearsall Community Primary School

MY JOURNEY TO THE SOUTH POLE

My journey has started,
To the South Pole,
It is so cold,
I want to go home.

I'm almost there,
I've got the flag,
Using huskies,
It's going so fast.

I'm at the South Pole,
I've planted the flag,
The huskies are tired
And so am I.

I'm on my way home
To my fire,
I am so glad
That I have succeeded.

Craig Roberts (10)
Hearsall Community Primary School

SPACE

Vaults out of bed and I jumped in my space kit
Off to Jupiter!
Yes, all my friends are here.
Ahh look, a little volcano!
Go back home and . . .
Eat all my dinner.
Sleep time for me zzz

Jibraan Tariq (9)
Hearsall Community Primary School

A Voyage Of A Football

I came,
Soaring over the pitch,
Ejected from a chip by the No.8,
Into control of the No.10.
Propelled sidewards,
Heading for the touchline,
Collected by a late lunge,
Catapulted into the other team's half.
Collected by the No.6,
Tackled from his feet by an early slider.
Dribbled 20 feet,
Passed rather clumsily,
Causing me to be intercepted by the No.7.
Robbed by a wild tackle from the No.8.
Plunged straight passed the keeper into the netting.
Goal! Goal! Goal!

William Ward (11)
Hearsall Community Primary School

A Cooking Book From Mars

I was reading a book on how to cook,
A page sprang up about cooking monsters.
I needed a feather from the bower bird from Mars,
Getting there I saw the bower bird from Mars,
So I squeezed his belly and then,
Everything exploded like jelly,
Out popped a gungie fellow,
By the name of Bungiele Bellow,
And in his hand was a feather from the bower bird from Mars,
I took it from his hand and went back to Earth.

Callum Peter West (9)
Hearsall Community Primary School

I HAD A DREAM, OH I HAD A DREAM

I had a dream, Oh I had a dream.
I was going to space.
I put my silver uniform on
I put my great boots on.
And now ready for blast-off,
3, 2, 1, *Boom!*
There, I was rising up and up.
Passing my city, passing my school,
Passing the bright blue sea.

I had a dream, Oh I had a dream.
I was having a nice time and relaxing
But then I accidentally pressed a button
I did not know what it was.
The spaceship started to shake
I closed my eyes then the shaking stopped.
I heard a bell and I woke up and found out
I was in bed and the bell really was my alarm clock.

Hannah Ahmed (9)
Hearsall Community Primary School

FLOATING

I was on a cloud.
In the sky.
The cars below were very loud.
It felt like I could fly.

It was very clear.
It was quite light.
Now I had no fear.
Soon it would be night.

Watching the stars.
The moon was very bright.
Watching all the cars.
What a beautiful sight.

Lauren McFadden (9)
Hearsall Community Primary School

COWBOYS AND RED INDIANS

Cowboys rounding up cows
Cowboys fighting the Red Indians
Cowboys on a long journey
Cowboys riding and shooting.

Red Indians scaring away the cows
Red Indians fighting cowboys
Red Indians hunting for food
Red Indians sleeping and snoring.

All of these people fighting
Oh! Look here it's a time machine
Everybody trying to get in
Two of each got in, let's go forward in time.

Here we go into the 1960s
Oh! There's a pretty hippie
Now into the '70s
Big programme Thunderbirds

1980s here we are
Everyone in pop was famous
1990s were dirt and mess everywhere.

Bring us back!

Ryan Peter Perry (10)
Hearsall Community Primary School

SPACE

Venus to Mars
Space
Shooting stars all around
Space
Rockets and planets
Space
Space stations and spaceships
Space
The dark, starry sky
Space
Time to go back
Here's the countdown
10, 9, 8, 7, 6, 5, 4, 3, 2, 1
Here I am
Back down at Earth
Everyone's cheering
My journey is complete
Space.

Robyn Knighton (10)
Hearsall Community Primary School

SATURN RING

I was on a voyage
To see the Saturn ring
But when we boosted the spaceship up
The spaceship started to sing.

First it sang Titanic
Then it tried to waltz
By now we were all thinking
There must have been a fault.

When the mechanics designed it
They programmed it to sing
But not to fly into space
Or to the Saturn ring.

Steven Woods (10)
Hearsall Community Primary School

HOT AIR BALLOON IN THE SKY

H ere we go on a journey round the world
O n a trip through the Universe
T ime ticks until it's time to go.

A t the beginning of the tour I can't wait to start
I think I might be a bit scared over the oceans
R ight, we're off to see the beautiful surroundings.

B egin the flight
A s we lift off, I'm very excited
L ift off!
L ook! All the people are like ants
O nly a few clouds above us now
O ne country gone out of sight
N ever going down.

I taly, Iran and India
N etherlands, Norway, even Nepal.

T here's Tunisia, Turkey or Thailand
H ey, there's Hungary and Honduras
E gypt, Estonia and Ecuador.

S pain, Sweden even Switzerland
K enya, Kuwait or maybe Kazahkstan
Y ugoslavia and Yemen, now we can all go home.

Stephen Hall (10)
Hearsall Community Primary School

MY VOYAGE WITH HARRY POTTER

M   et Harry Potter? I have,
Y   ou know about him?

V   oldamort's dead, both Harry and me, magicked
O   ff his head!
Y   ou read about him?
A   nd you should too, but I've met him,
G   et it? Take it you have too? 'No' I hear you say,
E   very day I see him, every single day.

W   e met at school, Oh what a school too,
I   t's very clean it is, even Hagrid's too!
T   he school's name I've forgotten, what is it now?
H   ogwarts, that's it! Here comes Krum, Oh wow!

H   ope Harry continues with his fame,
A   nd about his parents, Oh what a shame!
R   eading the fourth book? I am too,
R   eally good it is, yes, I'm talking to you,
Y   ou hear me now, right that is it!

P   retend I've met him? Not one bit!
O   ld Fogy Snape his lessons are dull,
T   urn him into a kid, maybe into a bull!
T   urn your switch to Quidditch rules!
E   very wizard has Quidditc h tools!
R   ead it now? Good, thanks pal!

Sam Goddard (11)
Hearsall Community Primary School

THE JOURNEY TO MARS

Starry galaxy
Purple planet
Ancient Jupiter
Curling twister.
Enormous rocket slung into hyper-space
Shiny Saturn, shining bright in the moonlight.
Fattest planet
Unusual menaces
Icy moon skating
Tiny Mercury.
Inky black
Opening sky
Naughty comets
Purple Pluto.
Opening rockets
Windy space
Enormous Mir
Rocky rocket
Shiny star
Tiny speck in space
Accident on Mir
Tiny stars
Icy Pole
Orange Sun
Naughty asteroids.

Jordan Christian (10)
Hearsall Community Primary School

SPACE VOYAGES

Space, space, space, how long does it go on for?
Days, days, days.
We look as if we're in the same place.
Stars, stars, stars continuously gleaming.
We, we, we are getting very star sick
Food, food, food we're eating all the same mush.

Fish, fish, fish all are different kinds.
Drink, drink, drink, we drink all of ye old rum.
Saturn, Saturn, Saturn, we finally made it.
Hurrah, hurrah, hurrah, we're going to the Saturn rings.

There, there, there are beautiful Saturn rings
Arh, arh, arh, let's all go and relax
Bye, bye, bye, we'll miss you a lot now.

Yashir Easterlow (10)
Hearsall Community Primary School

MY VOYAGE

M y dream is very tranquil,
Y ou'll enjoy it.

V enture with me on my ship,
O n the aqua sea we go,
Y ou can feel the swift current take you by,
A way over the sparkling ocean,
G liding along the water's surface,
E njoy it, it's only a dream!

James Hnatushka (10)
Hearsall Community Primary School

THE MOON CHILD

The moon child poked her head up
From beneath the horizon.
She smiled down upon the earth,
Watching, watching.
She shook her silver head,
Laughed her clear laugh,
People down on the earth,
Were smiling up at her,
She cast her bright silver light,
Over their heads,
Covering the world,
In moonshine.

Katie Lines (10)
Hearsall Community Primary School

PEOPLE ON THE STREET

People on the street
Kicking cars
Driving vans.
People on the street
Running around
What have they found?
People on the street
Nothing to eat
Walk on their feet
People on the street.

Ross Warner (9)
Hearsall Community Primary School

THE FROG YEARS

Small,
Soft,
Slimy,
Slippy,
Spawn.

Croaky,
frog

Tiny,
Thin,
Twisting,
Tadpoles.

Carnivorous,
Confused,
Incomplete frog.

Martha Pedler (9)
Hearsall Community Primary School

SEA VOYAGE

S   et out to sea,
U   sing their submarines,
B   ubbles coming out of the engines,
M   oney awaits for them,
A   tlantis will be found!
R   ight! Left! Left! Right!
I   n submarine, all is well,
N   o sight of Atlantis,
E   very year on the 5th August,
S   end out subs to find submarine.

Joshua Wood (10)
Hearsall Community Primary School

A VOYAGE TO HEAVEN

Sitting in a deckchair
watching blossom like tears
falling from heaven, pink and white tears.

A metaphor
Sapling growing,
Little girl growing.
Everything changes
New buds,
New leaves,
New blossom.
Everything changes
New growth,
New job,
New people.
Droopy tree,
Dark colours
Old, frail, fragile, delicate
Sweet smell of lavender

Closing her eyes for the last time, watching angels
flying up high, pink and white angels.

The world that she left sits and thinks of memories.
The whole world sits in silence and thinks of memories
Pink and white memories.

Charly Franklin (9)
Hearsall Community Primary School

MY VOYAGE OF SPACE

3 . . . 2 . . . 1,
Off we go,
For a voyage through space.

Through the ozone
Through the world's atmosphere,
And into space.

Everything was black except for the stars,
The moon was shining on the Earth,
All the planets in sight.

Mercury shining in the sunlight,
Venus having a shadow,
Earth fading as we look down.

Mars with a big crater,
Little aliens popping out,
Little water streams on it.

Jupiter and Saturn,
The biggest planets,
The rings of Saturn,
And amazing craters.

Meteors and comets,
Flying through the sky,
Looking for somewhere to go.

Neptune and Uranus,
Two lonely planets,
Moving around the sun.

Finally the space station,
On the planet Pluto,
Now the voyage in space is over.

Jamie Barnes (10)
Hearsall Community Primary School

STUCK IN TIME!

We're stuck in 1980
We don't know what to do
We have to find the time crystals
To get back to 2001
But we don't know where the crystals are
They are so hard to find
They could be in a paper shop
Or they could be down a mine
But we're nowhere near these things
We're 157,000 miles away.

Oh look I've found one
Right underneath my feet
It's the very first crystal
To get us back to Earth.

Two more crystals to go
They could be anywhere
They could be in the park
They could be in the air somewhere
Oh look! I've found another
The second crystal to get us back to Earth.

The last and final crystal
It has to be in here
I peeked out of the window, nothing
But then I saw a flashing light
It was my last crystal
I am now going back to Earth
Goodbye!

Matthew Duffy (10)
Hearsall Community Primary School

SPACE ODYSSEY

Lost in space,
Looking for a way back home,
We're in our ship,
All alone.

Lost in space,
Been travelling four years now,
We need to get back home,
But how?

Lost in space,
Our radar went blip
Something is firing,
At our spaceship!

Lost in space,
Heading to certain doom,
Oh no - that's a missile!
Kaboom!

Jake Cardwell (9)
Hearsall Community Primary School

ROCKET TO THE MOON

Vaulting towards the sky,
Out of my boring house,
Yes, I'm nearly there,
Ahh, I'm losing control,
Grabbing hold of the rocket,
Eventually I gained control,
Stars all around me sparkling
In the sky.

Daniel Hobbs (9)
Hearsall Community Primary School

WHEN I WENT TO FIND MY ISLAND

When I went to find my island
I ran away from home
I sailed my boat across the seas
To find my island.

When I went to find my island
I stopped at Lapland to say 'Hello!'
To a man called Santa Claus
Stopped off to feed the penguins.

When I went to find my island
It was tough but I got through it all
Sailed the seas
Still no sign of my island.

When I went to find my island
It didn't go very well
I decided just to go back home
With my family and friends beside me.

Jade Elliott-Archer (9)
Hearsall Community Primary School

SPACE

Space, black with twinkling stars,
Space, black with space fish going by,

'Bobble, bobble' is what they say,
Space, black with the Titanic going to Mars or Venus.

John Booker (10)
Hearsall Community Primary School

A VOYAGE IN SPACE

Flying in space in a spaceship
Seeing spiral galaxies flying past
I'm scared on my voyage in space.

Seeing Earth from a distance, Earth in space
Looking up at the stars in space
I'm joyous on my voyage in space.

Going past Mercury, going past Mars
Doing the moonwalk out in the stars
I'm enjoying my voyage in space.

Landing on the space station, unloading all the parts
Building up the space station
I'm exhausted on my voyage in space.

Coming back from the space station, back from space
Landing on Earth
My voyage in space is over.

Niall Coyle (10)
Hearsall Community Primary School

PIRATES

Swish, swash, swish, swash,
This is the sound of the waves,
We're going to the island the pirates say,
The treasure is in the caves.

'Quickly, quickly,' they said very fast,
'We are near the island
And pull up the mast!'

We found the treasure
And they all said 'Yippee!'
Swish, swish,
Let's go in the sea.

Thanks from my mates,
And from me,
When you are bored,
Just go to the sea.

Arrandeep Kaur (9)
Hearsall Community Primary School

SNOWFLAKE

A journey of the snowflake,
Gliding elegantly through the air
As it falls, it twists and turns
Floating like a trapeze artist.
Curving slowly through the air
Never stopping always wandering
A journey in search of the crisp, white blanket
It tumbles on, like a court jester.
But makes no sound
Drifting, diving and dropping.
Always searching
Never stopping
Its solo search
Has come to an end
The crisp, white blanket
Becomes its friend.

Aaisha Iqbal (10)
Hearsall Community Primary School

TRAVELLING THROUGH SPACE

My bright red spaceship
Travelling through space.
From Mars to Jupiter
Travelling through space.
Looking down at the stars seeing Mars
Travelling through space.
Shooting stars passing by
Planet to planet
Travelling through space.
I love space seeing things
Like shooting stars, Mars and Earth
Travelling through space.
Time to go back down to Earth
Ten, nine, eight, seven, six, five, four, three
Two, one, now I have seen space
I'm back from space
I know it was the best thing
Travelling through space.

Chloe Owen (10)
Hearsall Community Primary School

THE STRANGE DAY

I was in my balloon
when all of a sudden there was a huge gust of wind.
It was so big it blew me to a faraway land
with big chocolate balls, which I ate.
Then all of a sudden I was blown back home
to my mum and dad.

Reine Walker (9)
Hearsall Community Primary School

HOT AIR BALLOON

Hot air rising from the balloon,
Once we are so high,
The world looks so small,
Air is rising from the balloon,
I feel so scared, I'm flying,
Rising, rising, rising
Bouncing up and down,
All the birds look so big,
Flying in the air so high, so amazing, so scared,
Lifting higher and higher off the ground,
Once we reach the clouds, the world begins to get blurry,
Once to we begin to land,
Noon approaches, the balloon settles.

Beau Nash (10)
Hearsall Community Primary School

ICE CREAM

Ice cream, ice cream, oh how delicious it is,
Every time I'm not allowed it, I steal it from my friend Liz.

I'm so badly addicted to it that my mum thinks it's bad for my teeth,
My friends have already even nicknamed me the 'Ice cream Thief'.

There are dainty types such as Screwball and Solero
And even better ones like Zap and Mr Snow.

I reckon that ice cream is the best food ever
Whoever invented it must be very clever.

Ice cream, ice cream is ever so nice,
It is definitely better than curry and rice!

Sharanjeet Nijjar (10)
Holbrook Primary School

MEMORIES

Memories, memories, memories
We can't throw them away,
They keep coming back,
So we live them and don't say.

They remind us of good and remind us of bad,
They bring back thoughts,
They make us happy and they make us sad.

They are little reminders,
At the back of our head,
They remind us for we are their finders.

We can't forget them or ignore,
They stay there forever reminding,
To stop them there is no law.

Just what we think,
Is a memory,
Somehow we have to find the link.

Memories, memories, memories,
Not much we can do,
For they have a meaning too.

Memories, memories, memories,
They do as they please.

Shahreen Bashir (10)
Holbrook Primary School

BEST FRIENDS

Best friends, we shall remain.
Everlasting, we shall stay together.
Showing our friendship all the time is what we'll do.
Together, through bad times and good times.

Friends are friends you can rely on.
Remember one another throughout our lives.
In our hearts we'll always be best friends.
Supporting each other, we'll be best friends forever.

Never shall we break up.
Problems will not come between us.
Separation will never happen.

Everlasting, we'll stay together.
Every day we'll help each other.
Every second we'll think of each other.
Never share our secrets with anyone else.
Day by day, we'll always be best friends.
Best Friends Forever!

Rakinder K Kalsi (10)
Holbrook Primary School

PLAYING IN WATER

Children splashing
    Adults nattering
        Picnics waiting
            Babies babbling
                Ice cream melting
                    Children waving.

Fiona McCann (9)
Howes Primary School

MOON

The moon, the moon,
shines in the dark sky,
with the twinkling stars.

The moon, the moon,
is a still torch,
no wind, nothing at all,
just stillness.

The moon, the moon,
shines so bright,
up in the sky.

The moon, the moon,
dies out in the afternoon,
but it appears in the night,
shining even brighter.

Michael Stokes (10)
Howes Primary School

MY MONKEY AND ME

My monkey and me went to see the sea,
but the sea was sold,
to a man who was bold,
and the sea said 'Man do you want my gold?'
But my gold was sold,
to a man who was cold,
then sold again to a man who was old.
No one wants me I told you so,
You can have me
You cheeky monkey!

Claire Ell (10)
Howes Primary School

FIRST DAY AT SCHOOL

A million, billion miles away from home,
I'm going to meet my teacher soon!
What is a teacher?
It's probably the one who makes tea for everyone,
I suppose that's kind of fun!

Oh no, I have to see the head teacher now!
What is a head teacher?
It could be a head who drinks tea from the teachers
What am I going to do?

The bell goes, the secretary comes,
She's gone to get some coffee,
With hundreds of toffees!

She takes me to the glassroom
What is a glassroom?
Oh, I'm scared!
I know it's a whole room made of glass,
Wow! Just think of that!

A man shows me the library,
Whatever that is!
A woman shows me hundreds of books!
What are books?
Are they the books that give everyone evil looks?

We bump into the hair taker,
What is a hair taker?
I know! It's the man who takes everyone's hair!
No wonder that's why nearly everyone's got hardly any hair!

Hinel Lakhani (11)
Howes Primary School

PLAYING IN WATER

People dashing
    Water splashing
        Clothes dripping
            Children flicking
                Swimsuits soaking
                    Children moaning
                        Mummies rubbing
                            Daddies hugging.

Lorna Tweed (9)
Howes Primary School

IN GAMES

Children winning
        People singing
                Feet racing
                        Girls skipping
Whistle blowing
        Ball bouncing
                Friends playing
                      Squad moving.

Anna Doggett (9)
Howes Primary School

CHOCOLATE

Chocolate is scrummy
Tasty and yummy.

Wrapped in shiny wrappers
Nothing else matters.

Everybody likes it
With their shiny packet.

Three different flavours
Ready to do favours.

Samantha Lea (11)
Howes Primary School

THE FIRST VOYAGE TO THE MOON

Neil Armstrong was a traveller to the moon
It was not made of cheese so he didn't need a spoon.

At the time there was a great race
To be one of the first men in space.

He took off in a great rocket
It was a fabulous sight, so don't mock it!

Travelling through space, past all the stars he did fly
Many a time he thought this is so dangerous, I might die!

He floated in his room
As he came nearer the great moon.

Then his capsule did land
There upon the vast, empty sand.

He put his foot on the moon that day
Then said those most famous words that people still stay
'One small step for man
One giant leap for mankind'.

Roshan Bhairon (10)
Howes Primary School

WINTER!

It's winter now, it's cold and damp,
with frozen ponds and rivers.
The ducks and swans are unhappy
because they can't swim.
The wet and wild wintry breeze
and the snowy snowmen sneeze.
But winter is my friend
when it snows it doesn't snow on me.
When a snowflake falls and you hold it
it feels like you have got the whole winter in your hands.
It's winter now!

Alex Allen (11)
Howes Primary School

PLAYING FOOTBALL

People passing
Teammates shouting
Fans tutting
Crowd booing
Opponents losing
Best team winning
Trainers muddy
Dirty playing
Whistle blowing
Goalies saving
Strikers sighing.

Joe McCauley (8)
Howes Primary School

Wrestling - The Rock

The Rock - the people's champ will still stand after anything
like The Pedigree,
the choke slam.
The Rock will still stand.
The Rock, the most electrifying man in sports entertainment.
The Rock's word 'Oh Jubroni you're too bony,
go back to the gym you don't know me.'
If you smell what The Rock is cooking.

Usman Khan (11)
Howes Primary School

What Is Wrestling?

The ring is about fear, regret, blood, sweat and tears,
people putting their lives on the line.
Flying from one corner of the ring to the other.
Wrestlers looking for fame and glory
and wanting to be the champion,
all in the name of sports entertainment.

Colin McCann (10)
Howes Primary School

Snow

As the snowflakes fall softly in sprinkles
from the grey, misty sky.
Excitement fills the air
just waiting to play outside.
Snow bombs zooming through the air
like meteorites pounding the earth.

Laura Tipple (10)
Howes Primary School

QUIET NIGHT

The moon hangs in the black, velvet sky,
Stars glinting around it.
Wolves' cries echo the silence,
Trees whip each other in the night breeze,
Casting a silhouette against the moon.

Wings are spread and owls swoop,
Tiny feet scurry as mice run home,
Back to safety and warmth.

It had been a long, cold night,
And all was still.
As the warm embrace of the sun
Streamed through the window smiling at me.

Emily Honey (11)
Howes Primary School

CHRISTMAS

Christmas is my favourite day.
Hoping everything goes my way.
Ringing bells on Santa's sleigh,
Interesting food on display.
Special music starts to play.
Tree lights twinkle and ribbons sway.
Mince pies presented on a tray.
Angels sing while children play.
Santa's very special day.

Penny Woolley (10)
Howes Primary School

SAILING A LONG TIME AGO

The calling crowds call out to their friends
As the captain clambers aboard
Anchor's away as the ship's sails catch the wind
The sailors' shouts drown out the seagulls' cries.

Through the rough, raging seas, the battling bow of the ship
Slides and slips through the dark, deep, deadly seas.

Days and nights down below, the damp, dark decks
Dreaming of dangers that might lie ahead.

Sun rises, a call from the crow's nest
Land in the east, drop anchor, the journey ends.

Danielle Noble (11)
Howes Primary School

TORTOISE

Lumbering carefully over sand and water,
Eating, stumbling, groping blindly,
To his favourite place - Foodland.
His delicious food finished, now the full-up tortoise
Feels his way, one foot after another,
Choosing a path in the sloppy grass
Which feels to him like owls on top of his hard shell
Making heavy footsteps and trying very hard
The tortoise finds a sleeping place
Zzzzzzzzzzzzz

Tarnjit Kaur Bhambra (11)
Howes Primary School

MARS

The vast red plain
Stretching for miles
Black acid spurting out of mounds of rock
And a silence
Going on forever
Whilst dust whips over your feet.

A cold wind
Circling round you
A mysterious presence
Near, yet so far
And the moon
Smiling down at you.

Years seem like seconds on Mars
Time passes so quickly
You wouldn't know it was there
It is the silent planet
It is the red planet
It is Mars.

Francesca Kirtley-Paine (10)
Howes Primary School

SNOWMEN

Snowmen are big and fat,
with a tall, black hat
and their hair sticks out like a big, round mat.

Snowmen's eyes are cold and bare
and a big, long carrot nose
with a dotty smile
and it makes you happy too.

Andrew Bowell (11)
Howes Primary School

MOUNTAINS

Caverns old
Stories told.
Over hill, over dale
To lands dark and pale.
Harsh winds cold
Caverns old.

Where the wind blows
No one knows.
Tunnels going up or down
Softly draped in a cobweb gown.
Harsh winds cold
Caverns old.

The snow on top
If caused to will drop.
At the top the trip's almost done
And you're face to face with the glaring sun.
Harsh winds cold
Caverns old.

Hannah Kirtley-Paine (10)
Howes Primary School

PLAYING FOOTBALL

Players scoring
Referee whistling
Goalies saving
Players running
Red Card waving
Players fouling
Legs aching.

Kieran Orchard (8)
Howes Primary School

MY FIRST DAY AT SCHOOL

I remember my first day at school
I made my mum look like a fool
I tried to hold in the tears
And face my biggest fears.
The teacher took me by the hand
And led me to the sand.

I made lots of friends at school
We did assemblies in the hall
We went out to play
At the same time every day.
Most of the time the teachers shout
But that's what school is all about.

Shona Hands (10)
Howes Primary School

PLAYING IN WATER

Boats racing
Ducks splashing
Baths running
Hands washing
Rivers flowing
Frogs leaping
Rain falling
Fish swimming.

Lauren Smee (8)
Howes Primary School

A Pop Star's Poem

Britney Spears is very pretty,
and Bradley from S Club 7 is very witty.
Christine Aguilera has a mobile phone
to practise her singing tone.
Ronan Keating wears funny clothes
to go with his glowing nose.

Emma Bunton is a Spice
and Westlife are very nice.
Eminem is a rapper
Samantha Mumba is very dapper.
That is the end of my pop star poem
and now I am goin'.

Jade Kelly (10)
Howes Primary School

Playing In Water

Children laughing
Water splashing
Mums shouting
Time wasting
Waves flowing
Babies crying
Dads swimming
Boys sliding.

Natasha Jackson (9)
Howes Primary School

PLAYING IN WATER

People splashing
Water flying
Teachers shouting
Mothers watching
Children resting
Costumes soaking
Legs twirling
Children playing.

Mitchell Bailey (8)
Howes Primary School

PLAYING FOOTBALL

Boots kicking
Hands catching
Referee whistling
Players fielding
Crowd cheering
Hands throwing
Muscles aching.

Aaron Allen (8)
Howes Primary School

WAY HOME

T-shirt hanging
Children clinging
Mothers shouting
Boys fighting
Girls chatting
Babies bouncing.

Trisha Prajapati (8)
Howes Primary School

SCHOOL YEARS

On the first year of school
I saw the swimming pool.

On the second year of school
I learned all the rules.

On the third year of school
I thought it was pretty cool.

On the fourth year of school
I forgot about the rules.

On the fifth year of school
I acted like a fool.

On the sixth year of school
My friends were acting cool
but the year was nearly over
so I became a bother.

I hope you enjoyed this poem
because now it is over.

Michelle McLean (10)
Howes Primary School

PLAYING FOOTBALL

Game starting
Players scoring
Referee sorting
Goalies diving
Strikers passing
Fans shouting
Whistle blowing.

Dean Barlow (9)
Howes Primary School

PLAYING FOOTBALL

People passing
> Teammates shouting

Crowd booing
> Opponents losing

Best team winning
> Reds beaten

Trainers muddy
> Referee booking

Goalkeeper saving
> Supporters waving.

Hayden Ludford (8)
Howes Primary School

PLAYING FOOTBALL

Players running
Children studding
Referee sorting
Other team taunting
People fouling
All the crowd scowling
Whistle blowing
Pitch not flowing
Everyone going
Everyone gone.

Mark Coyles (9)
Howes Primary School

THE ALIEN

The alien was as round as the moon
Five legs he had
And his ears played a tune
His hair was purple
And his knees were green
He was the funniest thing I had ever seen
As he danced in the door
Of his strange spacecraft
He stared at me
And giggled and giggled!

Sonia Gherra (10)
Howes Primary School

PLAYING FOOTBALL

Players scoring
Referee sorting
Managers roaring
Supporters calling
Goalies diving
People arriving
Men racing
Feet pacing
Crowds raising
Everyone praising.

Kieran Merrick (9)
Howes Primary School

THE WITCH

The witch lives in a cave
Her name is Sabrina I think.
This is my description of her:
Curly hair knotted and dirty,
Yellow and black teeth
Ragged clothes as well.
She never comes out
Only to do her shopping.

Tasmin Mills (10)
Howes Primary School

PLAYING IN WATER

Children splashing
Dolphins diving
Lifeguards staring
Adults talking
Teachers shouting
People jumping
Children begging to stay
Come again another day!

Nicolette Bazeley (8)
Howes Primary School

THE SEA

The salty sea
The beautiful sea
Rushes at me
As I watch

The salty sea
Splashes at me
And sail boats
Sail the surf.

Zirah Khan (8)
Joseph Cash Primary School

TEN LITTLE CHILDREN

Ten little children
sitting in a line
along came a rattle snake
and then there were nine.

Nine little children
all very late
one got left behind
and then there were eight.

Eight little children
on holiday in Devon
one stayed behind on his own
and then there were seven.

Seven little children
building with bricks
one dropped one on his toe
and then there were six.

Jonathan Bentley (7)
Joseph Cash Primary School

THE SEASIDE

At the seaside
The sea splashed
The sun shone
Waves splish splashed
The surfers surfed
On surf.

Jordan Arrol (7)
Joseph Cash Primary School

BY THE SEA

At the seaside
The sea splashed
And the sun shone
The waves splashed and splished
As the surfers started to
Surf and slide.

Jack Downing (7)
Joseph Cash Primary School

ROBERT'S YOGHURT

There was a boy whose name was Robert,
Who made his own bubbling yoghurt,
To make it feel so very runny,
He added some milk and honey.
He took it off to school one day
And when all the children went out to play,
He left it by the staff room door
And it exploded all over the floor.

Elisha Henry (9)
Limbrick Wood Primary School

JACK'S SNACK

There was a boy whose name was Jack
Who made a huge, jumbo snack
By buying cheese and bits of ham
He finished off by buying lamb
He put it in a microwave
Then said . . .
'I know how I could save . . .'
But was interrupted by his sister Heather
Who would eat and eat and eat forever
He took it off to school one day
And when they all went out to play
He asked his best friend called Sam
'Do you want some of my ham?'
'Yes I do, we'll eat it here,
I'll make sure the coast is clear'
'There is nobody in sight, we're all alone,
Apart from the kid with the mobile phone.'

Jamie Elliott (9)
Limbrick Wood Primary School

ROB'S YOG

There was a boy whose name was Rob
Who made a yummy bubbling yog
He used ice soda, fruit and flour
And also added some sweet and sour
He took it off to school one day
And when the children went out to play
He left it near the staff room door
And when he came back there was no more.

Staci-Anne Dunlop (10)
Limbrick Wood Primary School

DEAN'S BEAN

There was a boy whose name was Dean
Who made a gigantic baked bean
By buying a few of Sainsbury's jars
And finished off by buying a Mars
He put it all together
And then came in his sister Heather
He took it off to school one day
And when they all went out to play
He left it in his shining locker
And off he went to play some soccer
At 3.30 he carried it home
And spotted some people building a dome
Then he saw a massive crater
And said 'I'll be back for that later.'

Sheridan Marshall (9)
Limbrick Wood Primary School

ROY'S TOYS

There was once a boy whose name was Roy
He made a plastic toy
Just for the fun and joy
Then he made a teddy bear
He had to use lots of hair
He took them off to school one day
And when they all went out to play
A quiet little boy called Ray
Had an idea to use some spray
The spray was bright yellow and blue
And then Roy came in and said 'Hey you!
That was going to win
But now it has got to go in the bin.'

Jade Neivens (10)
Limbrick Wood Primary School

MICHAEL DUNN'S B-B GUN!

There was a boy called Michael Dunn,
Who made a lethal B-B gun,
With metal pellets, little round balls,
They're very handy these kind of tools.
He took it off to school one day,
And when they all went out to break,
He started to shoot and they started to shake,
The teacher came out,
And was about to shout.
He pointed the gun at the teacher,
And shot, but the pellet just wouldn't reach her.
She picked it up,
And said 'Ay up.'
Michael said 'Excitement's what these people seek.
I will bring another one next week.'

Adam Johnson (9)
Limbrick Wood Primary School

CAT'S BAT

There was a boy whose name was Cat,
Who made a very hard wooden bat.
He used a bit of his dad's old wood,
And he wrapped it together, it looked quite good.
Then to make it feel so hard,
He put it in a tub of lard.
He took it off to school one day,
And when they all went out to play,
He went to hit a flour filled ball,
Which wasn't very funny at all.

Kieran Corbett (9)
Limbrick Wood Primary School

DANE'S HOME-MADE AEROPLANE

There was a boy whose name was Dane
He tried to make a paper aeroplane
He used plain paper and a bit of cane
Then to make it fly higher
He added a large tyre
He took it off to school one day
And when they all went out to play
He put it on the teacher's desk
While she was dealing with a pest
The pest was playing with the aeroplane
So Dane said 'Stop pest that is made out of cane
And he might break it'
So I told the pest to sit.

Naomi Boyfield (9)
Limbrick Wood Primary School

A MAN AND A PILL

There was an old man from Brill,
He took a dynamite pill,
His legs were tired,
The dynamite fired
And his ears shot over the hill.

Then he added a bit of towel
To make it taste a bit more foul.

Then he took it to work one day
And waited for someone to come and say
'Oh please may I have that little sweet?
I will come and massage your healthy feet.'

And when the man came back later,
He came and said,
'You little traitor.'

That was it for the man and pill,
So they got taken away by the Old Bill.

David Jennings (10)
Limbrick Wood Primary School

THE BOY FROM LEAMINGTON SPA

There was a boy from Leamington Spa
Who made a gigantic racing car
With lots of mechanical parts,
He then decided to add some darts.
To make it run even faster than ever,
He had an idea that was very clever.
By putting in a jug of water
With chlorine butter and a cup and saucer.
He drove it off to school that day
And when they all went out to play.
He left it in the teachers' lounge
And when the teachers all came in
They said, 'Oh my, what is this?'
They all were full of disgrace
And then the water blew in their face.

Kelly Munsey (9)
Limbrick Wood Primary School

DANE'S DAISY CHAIN

There was a boy whose name was Dane,
Who made a little daisy chain.
He made it out of smelly hay
And he sprayed it with some colour spray.
He took it off to school one day
And the teacher said 'Hip, hip, hooray.
Now where did you make that daisy chain?
You are crazy.
Why are you making a daisy?
Because you are lazy.'

Daniel Cooper (10)
Limbrick Wood Primary School

HORSES

Horses, horses, I love horses,
To have one is my wish.
Other people might like dolphins,
Rabbits, birds or fish.

Some are big, some are small,
Some are good, some are bad,
I don't have one at all,
This makes me sad.

I love horses, they are cute,
Riding them is good fun.
Cars go past and go toot, toot,
The horse keeps going, he's enjoying the sun.

Gemma Ahern
Little Heath Primary School

Happy Things

My happy brothers, are you there?
My happy cousins, are you proud?
I'm happy to see you proud, Dad,
And very joyful,
I'm very joyful.
My teachers are lovely,
Teachers are joyful,
Teachers are kind,
Teachers are cool.
Friends are good,
Some are lovely.
When my friends are over
To play with me,
I'm very happy.
When I go to my cousins,
They are kind to me
And play with me,
And it makes me happy!

Prabhjit Khera (8)
Little Heath Primary School

The Beach

The beach is as hot as toast.
The sand is as gold as the sun
And feels as soft as a baby's bottom.
The sea is as blue as the sky
And as cold as ice.
You can play and swim in the sea.
You can build sandcastles and bury your friends!
You can have a picnic and eat sandwiches,
You can get a tan and go brown all over.

Stacey Percival (9)
Little Heath Primary School

THE RAINFOREST

Today the animals are spending a day at the beach
so I decided to go with them.
They said they were going to save somebody
being animal caught by a man.
The man was nasty and fuffy.
He got away in a matter of time
but there was no way he was going to get away.
I had a boat.
Just in time we got our friend back.
That was never going to happen again.

Kimberley Louise Westlake
Little Heath Primary School

UNTITLED

Zombies are slow,
Boys and girls are fast,
Vampires are as dead as a rat.
At 12 o'clock, zombies come out,
Peek, pop they go.
We are nice, they are not,
They are dirty, we are not.
Mummies are slow as cats,
Cats were under the mat
When zombies ran.

Sarah May
Little Heath Primary School

FOOTBALL

The ball shot into the net,
The people stood on their feet,
When the referee blew the whistle
The crowd started to fight
About whether that should
Have been a goal,
But the ref allowed it
Because it would have started a riot,
Which the players would have got hit.
After the first goal they kept on coming
Until the other team scored,
Then they stopped coming until
The penalty shoot-out, when they
Won by the odd goal.
When they had finished, they
Started a fight on the way home.

Peter Masterson (10)
Little Heath Primary School

MY GOLDFISH

A goldfish is happy,
sometimes it is nasty.
It's got colourful skin
And gold, colourful fins.
When he eats his food,
He eats like a goon.

Tarnjeet Singh Sidhu
Little Heath Primary School

MY DREAM

Man United are my favourite team,
Playing for them would be my dream,
I wish I could play with Teddy Sheringham,
Playing with him would be my dream.

I wish I could play against Ronaldo,
Or if I could, play Rivaldo.
Playing against them would be my dream.

I wish I could play at the Nou camp
Even if it was too damp.
Playing there would be my dream.

Kieran Sheridan (10)
Little Heath Primary School

I AM HAPPY

I am excited when I go on holiday,
I feel wonderful when I see my kind friends,
I feel proud when I am kind,
I feel delighted when I play games.
I have some bright trainers,
I go to school,
There is a swimming pool,
I am very cool.
My brother is playing basketball.
I am happy,
I am snappy.

Blake Arthur (8)
Little Heath Primary School

My Best Friend

My best friend is kind.
In school he plays with me every day.
He is very cool as well,
But he is not a fool.

My best friend is fourteen.
In one year he will be fifteen
And sometimes when he swaps
Games with me, I like them. He's kind.

Every day when he comes out, he has
The ability to run fast and he is very naughty
In school and sometimes in his house.

When I go to his house,
His nasty brother and sister
Don't let me in,
But a friend in need is a friend indeed.

Rakesh Kumar (8)
Little Heath Primary School

If I Could

If I could I would build a time machine,
If I could I would play
For Man United,
If I could, I would fly,
If I could, I would be the king,
If I could, I would write down
Everything I would like to do,
But I can't!

Luke Arthur (9)
Little Heath Primary School

MY DREAM

I'd like to be a rocket man
And go into space.
I'd go to the moon
To see what's there.
I will see the clouds
And when I look down,
Little tiny houses.

Harsimran Singh Jutla (8)
Little Heath Primary School

MY DREAM

I want to be a cricketer.
I want to play cricket,
I want to bat.
I want to give
Poor people money,
I want to give
Hungry people food.

Kuljeet Mann (8)
Little Heath Primary School

MY FAT CAT

My fat cat comes to have a fight
And it comes out at night.
My fat cat plays football,
My fat cat scores.

Gurnake Atwal (8)
Little Heath Primary School

MY DREAM

I went in a balloon with beautiful colours,
A mad balloon.
I gave my pocket money to poor people.
If people cried I helped them.
I stopped them killing sharks for their fins.
I stopped them catching monkeys,
I stopped them killing tigers for rugs.
I listened to my elders,
There were no more homeless
Or hungry people on the streets.
I stopped them killing foxes for making coats,
No more killing snakes to make shoes.

Manvir Singh Nahal (8)
Little Heath Primary School

I FEEL WONDERFUL

I feel wonderful
In the golden sun,
The flowers are beautiful,
I feel fantastic.
I'm going to the excellent fair,
I feel so excited,
I think it's going to be groovy.
The rides are going to be superb,
The sweets are going to be scrumptious.

Navjeet Mann (8)
Little Heath Primary School

MY BEST FRIEND

My best friend is naughty,
My best friend is T,
He goes to school,
He hates bees.

He is a boy,
He is seven.
In four years
He will be eleven.

He's got a mum,
Her name is E.
He has a dad
Who always eats peas.

He has a friend
He says, 'Hi, hi.'
When it's time to go,
He says Bye, bye.'

Barjinder Bilg (8)
Little Heath Primary School

LIONS

Lions, lions are very strong,
Lions, lions get nothing wrong.
Lions, lions are good at art,
Lions, lions are very smart.

Kings of the jungle are they,
Kings of the jungle like to play.
Kings of the jungle like May,
Kings of the jungle block people's way.

They can stay as still as a bun,
They can run as fast as wind, they run,
Their back is as orange as hay, is their back,
Their nose is a dark, coal black.

Lions are the best!

Shindy Lall (9)
Little Heath Primary School

THINGS THAT MAKE ME HAPPY

When I'm at home I feel delighted,
When I'm at school I feel joyful,
When I get all my work right
I feel wicked and proud.
When I do PE I am excited and amazed.
When I share with people
I am really happy.
When the stars glitter
In the sky,
It feels lovely.
If the moon shines
Every night,
It feels cool.
When I read poems
I feel fantastic.
When the sun comes out
It's so bright and lovely.
When the people
Come out to play
I'm delighted.
When my mum and dad
Buy me toys,
I'm joyful.

Donna Townsend (8)
Little Heath Primary School

EVERYBODY MAKES ME HAPPY

My mum makes me happy when she picks me up from school,
when I get home she makes me hot chapaties,
While I'm giving my dad an enormous, super hug.
When I go to the temple I feel very excited,
When I do some work at the temple, I feel joyful and kind.
When I go on holiday, I miss all of my class,
Mrs Higginson, Mrs Tiplady and Mrs Khoza.
When I do hard work at school I feel ingenious and brainy,
When I go out play with my friends
I feel happy and fresh.
When I am at home and have a bath
I feel clean and wonderful.

Jasdeep Singh Sehmi (8)
Little Heath Primary School

MY PET PARADE

In my pet parade, I've got:

One enormous elephant,
Two domestic dogs,
Three cool cats,
Four racing rats,
Five miserable mice,
Six hissing snakes,
Seven slow snails,
Eight banana-mad monkeys,
Nine snow-coloured swans,
And ten dumb donkeys.

Chirag Bhatti (9)
Little Heath Primary School

MY DREAM

No more homeless people
No more people dying,
No more unhappy people,
I would like to be a pokémon.

Diviesh Jagatia (8)
Little Heath Primary School

AN IMPORTANT QUEST

If I were to go on an important quest,
I would surely go to another place.
I wouldn't bring that little pest,
I wouldn't want to see his face.

On my quest, I would be in China,
There will be a house to build
And things will keep getting finer,
There will be some people who surely will be killed.

And I would need to keep out my gun,
I'm feeling a little bit hungry,
I wouldn't mind a bun,
Oh no, the Indians are looking angry.

Bang, bang, bang! Hit, hit!
Yes! The Indians are dead.
They fell down in a pit.
Oooh, I hit one in the head.

I am now in Washington DC,
I can even hear a pin drop.
Where could the President be?
There he is, he's on the top.

Darby Harris (9)
Manor Park Primary School

ST VALENTINE

S   t Valentine's is a special day,
T   ea together and kiss till May.

V   alentine cards look beautiful with hearts
A   nd when dogs are in love they bark and bark.
L   ove is in the air.
E   njoy Valentine's day Tony Blair.
N   ine days to go and you love someone really badly.
T   oday is the day, but no one gives you a Valentine.
I   do not know why they don't love me, tell me please,
N   ow somebody's that's strange, but anyway there's my keys I
E   njoyed it of course, I got a girlfriend.
     How about you?

Tom Cain (8)
Manor Park Primary School

ST VALENTINE

St Valentine's day is very gay,
Together we'll kiss on that day.
Very happy, we'd make a good pair,
A lovely new house and a baby called Claire.
Lovely roses I'll send to you,
Each one so fresh, bright and new!
Now we don't sit and sob,
Together we'd be, just you and me, Bob!
Infinite kisses wouldn't be bad,
No not at all, it wouldn't make me sad.
Everybody's eating chocolates and watch out,
They could be bad.

Anthony Poole (8)
Manor Park Primary School

RAIN

Cold winds blowing,
It's freezing cold.
Tiny droplets from the roof,
Here comes the rain.
Rush inside,
Get the big umbrella.
Put your raincoat on,
Oh no, mine's gone!

Rain, rain, I hate rain
Dribbling down the windowpane,
Plip, plop, drip, drop,
Rain is falling all around me
You just look, then you'll see.
Look, I'm soaking wet!
I'm not drenched, not just yet.

Amy Andrews (9)
Manor Park Primary School

ON THE BEACH

On the beach,
Enjoying the gentle sea,
Having fun,
All the housework's done.
Sunbathing when the sun rises,
The real time to spend with your kids.
Going splish-splash in the cool sea,
Ice cream melting in your hand.
The best thing of all is
You can have peace and quiet
(And a bit of relaxation!)

Jusreen Sangha (8)
Manor Park Primary School

St Valentine

S   t Valentine's day is special in a way,
T   ry not to give the secret away.

V   ases with flowers in show people you love them,
A   nd then go up to the person and hug them.
L   ove, great love is what it's about,
E   verlasting love cannot make you shout.
N   ice people are even better,
T   ry not to rip their heart-shaped sweater.
I   nvisible love is still just as good,
N   ice if you knit the person a red, loving hood.
E   veryone likes Valentine's day!

Emily Flynn (8)
Manor Park Primary School

Saint Valentine's Day

Soon the special day will come, tomorrow is the day.
Time to open the letter and see who sent it away.
Valentine's the day.
A beautiful red rose has been sent to you,
Love from your admirer who wants to kiss you,
Enjoy the sweets he sent you.
Now it's your turn to give him something.
Your admirer is coming to your house.
You think, 'No, it's a trick.'
Now this poem has come to an end.

Amani Bone (8)
Manor Park Primary School

O GENIE

O Genie, Genie, Genie, O Genie,
I wish I could fly, fly in the sky
With the blackbirds, bluebirds, sparrows and magpies.

O Genie, Genie, Genie, O Genie,
I wish I could cook steak cake or
Maybe the biggest, tastiest meat pie
The world has ever seen. Yum, yum!

O Genie, Genie, Genie, O Genie,
I wish for a bunny, long-eared and funny,
So I can feed him and play with him
And much, much more.

O Genie, Genie, Genie, O Genie . . .
Aaarrrgh! All of your three wishes are up.
O no!

James Brown (9)
Manor Park Primary School

MUM AND DAD

My friends can be horrible,
My friends can be nice,
But when I'm down, at least I know I have you,
Mum and Dad, you're wonderful.
You are always there
To feel what I feel when I'm hurt.
You take the pain and stand as me,
Mum and Dad, I love you!

Rachel Franklin (9)
Manor Park Primary School

St Valentine

S	pecial people kiss all day
T	ime tonight, the gift will come.

V	alentine is the greatest of the year,
A	lways I will love you.
L	ove is in the air,
E	at all day with chocolates,
N	uts are with me and you,
T	ime you will be with me,
I	am keeping my love for you,
N	obody is getting my boy,
E	ver and ever I will love you.

Anna Johnston (8)
Manor Park Primary School

St Valentine's Day

S	pecial people kiss all day,
T	ry to make me happy.

V	alentine's cards,
A	ccept the cards you might get,
L	ovely chocolates may come to you,
E	at all the food you can get,
N	ear your Valentine you may kiss,
T	aste your food,
I	mprove your love,
N	obody is better than you,
E	very day I will love you.

Ashleigh Davies (8)
Manor Park Primary School

ST VALENTINE

S   ecret admirers are everywhere!
T   hank you for the chocolates.

V   alentine's is loving day,
A   ll people love someone,
L   ove is in the air,
E   ach and every creature on Earth loves something,
N   uts about you,
T   o love you as much as possible,
I   love you,
N   o one can love the way I love you,
E   ven elephants love each other.

Connor McGrath (8)
Manor Park Primary School

ST VALENTINE

S   weet smelling roses are so red,
T   rying to make your love happy.

V   alentine's hearts are red and shiny,
A   sking 'Will you marry me?'
L   ove is in the air,
E   njoying a kiss all night long.
N   ow is the time I want to kiss you,
T   hinking about you every day,
I   nstead of her, why not me?
N   ib of the fountain pen writing your first love letter,
E   ach day I will miss you.

Georgina Oag (8)
Manor Park Primary School

ST VALENTINE

S weet smell of people sending roses,
T reats of chocolate and roses.

V alentine cards arriving through the post,
A re you happy, because I love you.
L ove is going around the world,
E njoy Valentine's, February 14th.
N othing is more beautiful than you,
T hank you for the chocolates,
I love you,
N ever run away,
E ven you are so handsome.

Chanice Mancini (8)
Manor Park Primary School

THE GREATEST BUSY BEE

If I was a busy bee
I would buzz around the world.
I would be black, yellow
And all sorts of colours.
I would be the most beautiful thing in the world.
Could I make some honey?
I could even be the world's greatest busy bee.
Would I be the leader of the gang?
Should I be the biggest bee?
Will I be the biggest bee?
Will I get to be the world's greatest busy bee?

Emily Sherwood (8)
Manor Park Primary School

THE SNAKE

I am a slippery, silent, stealthy, strong, super snake.
People often make the mistake, I am not a garden rake,
I am not a pole, but I wear a hood. Yes, I am a King Cobra.

Fear me, flee, fly if you can because my only goal is to have some tea.
Don't give me a chance, go run, if you don't you're dead.
You won't be alive, you'll be my tea instead.

Other snakes envy me and hate me,
But I just say to them
'Don't be bad or you won't be my mate.'

Just listen to me, I'm like a poison machine,
I pump up my poison and then and there I'm mean.
Bite goes the poison machine, an injection of poison right into you.

Three or four seconds, there goes you.
At last I am happy, I got my tea,
Now at last I can sleep, byeeeeeeeeee.

Edward Kimberley (10)
Manor Park Primary School

WINTER

W indy days start in October, snow comes drifting down.
I   'll play in the snow and make a mini igloo, with ice as the
                                                    water freezes.
N ice, playful snow is what I need to have a snowball fight.
T all trees fall because of the wind, sometimes breaking glass.
E verything freezes because of the wind. (I get frozen too.)
     It's almost the end of the winter, hooray!
R est at last is all I want because I am frozen solid.

James Askew (8)
Manor Park Primary School

COVENTRY CITY!

When I wrote this poem,
Coventry City were yet again at the bottom of the table,
Struggling to survive the drop.
I meet Gordon Strachan down in our local pub,
When I tell him, 'Why don't you go back to easy training?'
And he says, 'What, like . . . my team of eleven against
                                      eleven dustbins?'
'Yeh, that could do the job,' I said.
'Yeh, right.'
'For heaven's sake, just give it a go!'
'Okay, okay, meet me at ten at the Ryton training ground
                                    on Wednesday,' he said.
I did what he said.
When I got there, he had already set them out
In a 4-4-2 position.
We played rubbish and lost eleven-nil.

PS: I support Cov!

Jake Spencer (8)
Manor Park Primary School

THE SPOOKY BEDROOM

I went up the stairs,
It was creepy,
The stairs were rattling,
I was afraid, then I heard a voice,
I thought it was a ghost.
I was too scared to turn the light on,
I wasn't going upstairs!

Stephanie Lambell (8)
Manor Park Primary School

COLOURS IN THE WORLD

I have a black cat called Quadriped,
I have some fish and they are gold,
My heart is red.
The tree trunk is brown.
Our school is bright green
And everything has its own colour.

Vincent Marzetti-Cook (8)
Manor Park Primary School

COLOURS

Pink is the colour of flowers,
Red is the colour of roses,
Blue is the colour of bluebells,
Yellow is the colour of buttercups,
Green is the colour of leaves,
Orange is the colour of geraniums,
Purple is the colour of pansies.

Louise Faulkner (8)
Manor Park Primary School

MY FRIENDS

I have got a friend called Tom.
He is my best friend. Tom likes pokémon.
Tom's favourite colour is yellow.
When I go round to his house,
He's always naughty.
We go to watch 102 Dalmatians.

Lauren Tighe (8)
Manor Park Primary School

The End Of The Rainbow

There's the rainbow,
The pot of gold,
Come on, let's go
Through the bushes,
Through the trees,
Over the fields,
All of us run!

Will we be rich?
I don't know.
When will it end?
I don't know.
How long will it take?
I don't know.

Then we wade
Through the dirty river,
Soon I get cold,
It's getting dark.
We're still not tired,
We're still strong,
But I'm getting sleepy.
Oh no, the rainbow's gone!

Francesca Rigby (8)
Manor Park Primary School

Untitled

Dragons roaring
on an island
in the middle of the sea.

Bees buzzing
in their hive,
(where they should be).

Me working
on a story,
this is not me.

Marie Low (8)
Manor Park Primary School

SCHOOL TRIPS

School trips are boring,
Why can't they be fun?
I would rather eat loads of chocolate buns!
Why can't we go places . . .
Mars or even the stars?
Pluto would be the best!
You wait and see . . .
I would eat the ground
And turn around,
I would make friends with aliens
And they would make friends with me!

If I could make friends with an alien,
I would choose a
Green one, a . . .
Big one, a . . .
Hairy one, and
Don't forget, a scary one!
Hee, hee, hee!
That tells us that we can
Make friends with anybody,
No matter who they may be.

'Hey kids, we are going to the park!'
See what I mean?

Bethan Schofield (9)
Manor Park Primary School

SEASONS

Winds blow, snow falls,
Icicles dangling from walls.
Never have I seen the floor so white,
This time though, it is quite bright,
Even though it's melting away,
Really enjoyed it every day.

Sun's shining so brightly,
Pink flowers glow lightly,
Running children playing in the park,
I'm just sitting in the dark.
None of us are feeling glum,
Great time in the sun.

Sun's beaming on the floor,
Underneath our front door.
My mum is sitting on a stool,
Me and my sister in the pool,
Everyone's feeling glad,
Running and jumping on their dad.

At autumn time, leaves fall
Underneath our football.
Tell me what colour the leaves are
Underneath our car.
Many leaves fall around,
No green leaves on the ground.

Dale Brogan (9)
Manor Park Primary School

SPACE

I wish I was a spaceman
So I could see space.
The dark, black sky with stars all around me,
People think the sky is blue, but it's black,
I want to go to space
So I can see monsters in space.

Catherine Frankton (8)
Manor Park Primary School

STRAY CAT AT NIGHT

When the night creeps over land,
Like a giant, enormous, mighty hand,
The stray cat comes out to try and seek,
The mice that daren't take a peek.

Suddenly, the cat spies upon the ground,
A little mouse playing around,
The cat's eyes grow wider every minute,
Waiting for the chance to pounce and kill it.

The cat creeps closer, still staring,
At the mouse who really was quite daring,
To be playing out at this time of night,
It would give the other mice quite a fright.

The cat then stops, and bows down low,
Waiting, waiting for the chance to go,
He suddenly leaps very high in the air,
And snatches the mouse, not missing a hair.

The poor mouse struggles to get out of its claws,
But the dangerous predator clamps down its jaws.

Daniella Da Silva (10)
Moseley Primary School

I REMEMBER!

I remember, I remember,
My nan before she died.
I always at on her garden wall,
When she was making strawberry pies.
My nana was short, not tall,
She was always smiling and happy,
But then my granddad died,
And that's what made her snappy.

I remember, I remember,
My nan before she died.
I will always remember her house,
And the games we played inside.
She always kept a huge teddy
For when I came to stay,
But I never got to say goodbye,
And that's what made me unhappy,
But I will always remember you Nanny!

Alison Hagyard (10)
Moseley Primary School

MUMMY REMEMBER

Mummy remember,
Someone, somewhere, dreams of your smile
And whilst thinking of you says life is worthwhile,
So when you are lonely, remember it's true,
Someone, somewhere, is thinking of you.

Love from your special little boy.

Mark Taylor (8)
Moseley Primary School

MOSELEY PRIMARY

M otor cars pour in through the gate,
O wen starts to communicate,
S ophie runs into school,
E asy-going she is, people say you need a pool,
L ovely going, Neil,
E nds an appeal,
Y ou only need a real note.

P romising teachers come to vote,
R obert says when it's playtime,
I magine a lovely playtime, but it's time for crime,
M ary Robinson comes to play,
A ll she thinks is hay,
R icardo Rikki comes to say
Y o Moseley, it's okay!

Robert West (11)
Moseley Primary School

MY PET MILLY

M illy is my pet,
Y ou'd think she was ordinary.

P erhaps she came from space,
E xtraordinary, extra-terrestrial is my Milly,
T wo pounds, that's all she cost.

M illy's my best friend,
I ntergalactic she may be,
L ove's only important to her and me,
L ong last friendship between her and me,
Y ou may think she's strange, but anyway, she belongs to me.

Sophie Reddington (10)
Moseley Primary School

I'M ALONE UNDER THE BED

It's dark under here
a spider's coming near.
I'm alone under the bed.

There's cardboard boxes
and paper planes.
I'm alone under the bed.

Old photos and things
school books, plastic bags.
I'm alone under the bed.

Old pens, old toys,
dirty socks, pen cartridges.
I'm alone under the bed.

Old pages from books,
coat hanger hooks.
I'm alone under the bed.

Pens, crayons,
pencils and tops.
I'm alone under the bed.

Sweater tops,
and cotton shorts.
I'm alone under the bed.

Woollen mitts,
saggy blue coats.
I'm alone under the bed.
Dolls' heads,
toy cars, missing wheels.
I'm alone under the bed.

All that used to be there,
but now it's all gone.
Only now I am truly alone.

Jennifer Bowers (11)
Moseley Primary School

WINTER POEM

The flowers are sleeping,
The trees are bare,
Leaves of all sizes everywhere.
A happy new year has just begun,
So sing this song, sing this winter song.

Animals are hibernating
All cosy and warm,
Bundled up as a bug in a rug.
A happy new year has just begun,
So sing this song, sing this winter song.

Icicles hanging from windows all cold,
The roads and paths are all slippery and icy,
But the sun is still bright in the sky.
A happy new year has just begun,
So sing this song, sing this winter song.

Home from school on a winter's night,
When it's dark and not bright,
But at home it's warm and nice.
A happy new year has just begun,
So sing this song, sing this winter song.

Victoria Heggie (8)
Moseley Primary School

MEN AND WOMEN RECIPE

Ingredients:

10 spoonfuls of blood,
8 pairs of bleeding eyes,
50 shot bullets,
2 pairs of Spanish noses,
1 chopped head (keep the brain)
5 chopped hands,
100 dead men and women.
(Make sure you have a cauldron of boiling water.)

First put in the 10 spoonfuls of blood,
Add 50 shot bullets,
Mix 2 pairs of Spanish noses,
Beat in 100 dead men and women.

Leave to boil for an hour,
Take out the 100 dead men and women,
Leave them to dry.
If they stick together, chop them in half.

Include one chopped head and keep the brain for flavour,
Carefully put in 5 chopped hands.
(Make sure that they don't choke you to death.)
Stir in 8 pairs of bleeding eyes.

Mix it altogether,
Leave for 30 minutes,
Take out of the cauldron and there you have it,
Your Dead Men And Women Soup.

Kieran Cunningham (11)
Moseley Primary School

OUT OF THE WINDOW

I sit and stare out of the window at eight o'clock at night
I wonder if it's night or is it pollution blocking up my sight.

I cannot see trees, only factories blocking up the sight
Of what was once green land that got stamped on by pollution
one night.

I sit and stare out of the window at the ruined world
And wonder what will be left for my children.

Emily Gill (9)
Moseley Primary School

THE NIGHT SKY

Up high in the night sky,
Hunter's moon shines like a diamond ring,
The stars gleam like moonlight,
Reflecting off the dark blue sea.
All the white clouds suddenly turn a dark, dark blue,
As the blood-red sun sets, the diamond moon rises,
Couples in love walk happily under the beautiful, night sky,
Eventually the night is over and the sun rises
For a smashing new day.

Neelam Patel (10)
Moseley Primary School

THE SUPREME STORM

The wild storm rages like an angry giant,
Screeching lightning bolts fly through the night sky,
Like fiery weapons and its thunderous voice bellows,
And echoes furiously.
The wind howls and shrieks irritatingly,
With its icy and slippery grip to the house,
As tightly as a metal clamp.
The rain beats horrendously against the window,
When the fire greets us like a mean lion.

Junaid Duberia (10)
Moseley Primary School

A LITTLE KITTY CAT

I have a little kitty cat,
Smokey is her name,
She likes to run from this to that
When she plays her game.

She's very cuddly and furry too,
And likes to hide within my shoe.
She chases a ball across the floor,
It's the funniest sight you ever saw.

She is so small,
I love her so,
She is always scratching
My big toe.

Samantha Pepper (8)
Moseley Primary School

MY DAD LEFT

I remember, I remember,
The saddest time of my life.
My mum was screaming,
My dad was shouting,
No longer man and wife.
I was sad,
My mum was glad,
My dad had left us all.
I remember, I remember,
James didn't mind because it wasn't his dad,
Me and Aimee were really sad.
I wish he would come back,
But my mum would give him the sack.
When my dad does come back,
Andy will be lucky if he doesn't get a whack,
I think she should definitely have him back.

Olivia Bartlett (10)
Moseley Primary School

TEACHERS

Teachers, all they do is
Moan, moan, moan!

I can't take it anymore!
Six hours a day all they do is
Groan, groan, groan!

And I am definitely sure
Will someone put an end
To all this
Groan and moan?

Abby Williams (9)
Moseley Primary School

MY VERSION OF 'THE OWL AND THE PUSSYCAT'

They set off that day and sailed away
Right over the deep blue sea.
In the end of the boat, a shark in a coat
Sat watching them, gleefully.
'Oh honey . . . the shark . . .
Before it gets dark,
Let's ask him a favour to do.
We'll offer him money
And some of our honey,
If he'll marry me, dear, to you,
To you, to you,
If he'll marry me, dear, to you!'

Reuben Kelly & Mia Abbot (10)
Moseley Primary School

THE PERSONIFICATION OF FOOTBALLER JAKE

I'm a footballer,
My name is Jake,
I'm a dirty little dog
And look at the money I make.

I wear really fancy clothes
And everybody knows
That I'm just the best.
PS: I don't wear a vest.

I like to eat
A lovely bit of minced meat,
Because that's my favourite,
It really is my favourite.

Kiran Kaur Bal (10)
Moseley Primary School

PLAYGROUND BULLIES

In the playground we all play games
In the playground they call us names.

In the playground where they run about
In the playground they scream and shout.

In the playground they punch and kick
In the playground is where they used to spit.

In the playground they wrecked our games
In the playground the teacher came.

In the playground the bullies became chickens
In the playground they were due for a metaphoric kicking.

In the playground the teacher said
'Come here boy and stop this instant.'

In the playground peace returned
In the playground I returned.

Mariam Khan (10)
Moseley Primary School

MOTHER

M y mum is kind,
O ther times, she's cross,
T here are times when she shouts,
H er face goes red and her
E ars go red and you need to
R un away!

Jane Townsend (8)
Moseley Primary School

SAD BALL

I am tired of getting kicked around,
All I can hear is a whistling sound.
After a while, I get hit in the back of the head
With a sized ten boot.
I am glad when the half-time whistle hoots.
The players come back on after a five minute break,
In three seconds I am as flat as a pancake.
I get kicked around like a blind old mole,
In 25 minutes Man U score a goal.
Cole gets his 17th goal and I am in
The back of the net like a dirty lump of coal.

Thirty-five thousand Coventry fans mad,
Man U fans are happy and glad.

Owen Davies (10)
Moseley Primary School

THE CAT

Seeking, staring, stalking prey,
Slowly, swiftly, ready to pounce.
Piercing the darkness with its claws
As sharp as Swiss army knives,
Slashing, piercing the skin
As if it was nothing.
Biting, chewing, like a savage beast,
Squealing thing shouting for help.
This was a very bloodthirsty battle,
Finally it drops slowly to the ground.
Finally the mayhem has stopped
And its unsuspecting victim
Is now dinner for the cat!

Samuel Farrington (11)
Moseley Primary School

WHERE'S THE PAINT?

I've found the brush,
I've found the paper,
I've found the classroom art table!

I've found the apron,
I've found the water,
I've even been to the toilet!

But the only thing I haven't found is the paint!
Where is the paint?
I've looked over here
I've looked over there
I just can't find the paint anywhere!

I asked the teacher,
'Look, it's right under your nose,' she said,
'Now let's draw your little creature.'

Nicole Whitlam (9)
Moseley Primary School

VALENTINE'S

St Valentine's, St Valentine's
Everyone loves St Valentine's

Flowers like roses and daffodils
Chocolate smooth and rich

Kisses and hugs
That's what I love

St Valentine's, St Valentine's
Everyone loves St Valentine's.

Cortney Dry (11)
Moseley Primary School

TEACHERS!

Teachers always make rules,
Rules! Rules! Rules!

Teachers always make us read,
Read! Read! Read!

Teachers always give us homework,
Homework! Homework! Homework!

Teachers always make us do geography,
Geography! Geography! Geography!

Teachers always make us do RE,
RE! RE! RE!

Teachers always make us do English,
English! English! English!

Teachers always make us do work!
Work! Work! Work!

Teachers always make us play games,
Games! Games! Games!

But teachers can't tell us what to do
At the weekend!

Sheena Patel (9)
Moseley Primary School

SPRING

Flowers are sitting in the field
As silent as can be,
The sun in the sky, saying 'Hi'
Then the flowers jump with happiness.

Birds singing in the sky,
Making children dance joyfully.
Then the children run in,
Because the rain starts to come,
Like leaves falling from trees.

Zoe Holmes (10)
Moseley Primary School

DINNER LINE

The line is gigantic,
It doesn't look romantic,
Actually it looks kind of sick.
People punching and kicking,
People are kissing,
I'm not looking,
No way josé,
I liked it the normal way
When people were standing straight.

James Bryson (9)
Moseley Primary School

A FRIEND

A friend is a friend,
The friend is mine,
You are that friend,
That is nice,
If you are the friend,
That is nice,
Then you are that friend,
That is mine.

Emma Sexton (8)
Moseley Primary School

THE SEA

The sea rocks near and far
It crashes hard upon the rocks
That turn over ships
And carries the froth to and fro.
Washing away the muddy sand
Bringing messages upon the land.
You can smell it, it smells like salt
It is home for sealife
And some are doomed
With pollution and litter.
The sea is useful.

The sea is tough and rough
It can be a giant
That tumbles over you
It goes in your mouth and makes you sick
You go surfing, you go out too far,
Nobody there, no help.
The sea is full of jellyfish
Some poisonous, some not
The sea is deep, you may drown
It rocks, throwing things around
The sea is dangerous.

The sea is good to relax
To swim and to dive
To touch nearly extinct sealife
It can be warm, it can be cold
The sea is clear, the sea is not clear
The sea is fun.

Jamie Randle (10)
Moseley Primary School

ME

My mum says I look like a giraffe
But when I tell my friends they all laugh
They say I look more like a bat wearing a pink, spotty hat
My sister says I look more like a monkey
But I say eating bananas is funky
My brother says I look like a big moth
And that I should wash my face with a big cloth
My teacher says I look like a bee making honey
But I told her straight away that wasn't funny
I've asked people if I'm a hare
And they've said yes, but I don't care
Because I'm happy being a big, growly bear.

Kevin Corbett (9)
Moseley Primary School

GLIDING

I sit and wonder,
It feels like I'm drifting,
Hovering high . . . high . . . high,
Above the clouds.
I'm in bottomless trouble,
I wonder, can anyone see me?
It's weird . . . I can't stop grinning,
At the same time I beam guiltily
Down on the city I've evaporated.
I'm in trouble . . . deep trouble,
But wait, I forgot,
No one can see me . . .
'I'm dead!'

Sakinah Hassan (10)
Moseley Primary School

TEACHERS

Teachers can be mean
Teachers can be nice
They can be fat, they can be lean,
And they might just get scared of mice.

Teachers can be vile
Teachers can be thick
They might even walk a mile
But you better not take the mick.

Teachers can be mad
Teachers can moan
They might even be your mum or dad
But they end up happy, when they go home!

Lijana Vesna Kaziow (9)
Moseley Primary School

SUN

Sun, sun, sun, let's have fun.
Run, run, run in the sun.
Lick, lick, lick, I'm licking a lollipop stick.

Sea, sea, sea, that's where I like to be.
Sand, sand, sand, let it run through my hand.
Happy days in the sun, I am having lots of fun.

Ashley Paul Rushton (10)
Moseley Primary School

FRIENDS!

Miss, my friend
Is treating me horribly
What shall I do?

Do what you want
Run away to Africa
It's no good asking me.

Miss, my friend
And I like each other now
I'm really happy.

Oh that's good
Get on with your work now
Your friend is waiting for you.

Elena Walker (9)
Moseley Primary School

NIGHT

Jagged white lightning
Muffled winter nights
Icy, frosty lakes
Starry, snowy nights
The moon floats on a glass lake
Mist rising from the banks.

Melissa Jacobs (10)
Moseley Primary School

A WINTER WALK

The wild storm rages like an angry giant,
Flashing lightning bolts through the sky like fierce weapons,
As its thunderous voice bellows and echoes furiously.

The wind shrieks loudly like an annoyed teacher.
Its icy pair of hands gripped the house as tightly as a rope.
Noisily the rain beats heavily against the windows.
Inside the fire greets us like a loving mother,
We feel as warm and snug as a teddy by the fire.

Gemma South (11)
Moseley Primary School

SPRINGTIME FLOWERS

Flowers are blooming,
Swaying slowly in the breeze,
With fragile petals,
Now it is spring.

Water flows downstream,
Shimmering in the sunlight,
Bubbling past flowers,
Now it is spring.

Beautiful flowers
Bring colours into our life,
I do love spring.

Victoria Chandler (10)
Moseley Primary School

THE FOOTBALL CRUMBLE

A pint full of mud
12 football players
200 football fans
1 football
Half of the grass on the pitch
25 cheese and onion pasties (half eaten)
30 steak and kidney pies
70 packets of Walkers crisps
1 broken leg
11g of sweat
6 sweaty kits
Gas mark 5

Add 11g of football sweat
then drop a pinch of grass
to add colour to sweaty football kits
put one bleeding broken leg in (and stir well)
leave for two minutes on gas mark 5.

Take out of oven
add half eaten cheese and onion pasties
70 packets of Walkers crisps
30 steak and kidney pies
spread thickly with some gooey mud.

Last of all, 200 football fans
and 12 footy players to eat it
to top it off, a football on top.

Sophie O'Hagan (10)
Moseley Primary School

THE SPACE RACE

We're up in Mars,
I can see the stars.
I am running too,
I can hear aliens shouting 'Whoo'.

Little green people running round wild,
I cannot see one human child.
I must be the only human,
There's people coming round saying, 'I'm the *Boo man!*'

The race starts at a green and blue line,
Everyone must be on time.
There's people crying, 'Wait for me,'
And people saying, 'Hee, hee, hee.'

I want a chocolate bar,
But I haven't got a spare car,
And there isn't a shop in sight,
And it feels like it's nearly night.

Then all of a sudden we hear 1 . . . 2 . . . 3 . . .
I can hear shouts, 'Whoo, hee, hee, hee,'
Then comes *bang!* And off we go.
There was an alien called Po!
I'm in the lead,
I'm going full speed.
Look out, here I come,
Oh no, that's my mum.

I'm coming to the finish line,
When I've finished we're going to drink white wine.
I turn the bend,
I'm at the end.

Yeah, finished.

Yes! I've won!

Vikki Rogers (11)
St Benedict's RC Primary School

THE SPACE RACE

There is a space race soon.
Neil Armstrong is entering,
Hopefully they will see the moon.

There are two countries entering the race,
Russia and the USA,
They will all run at their own pace.

There will be a festival or celebrations,
With activities for everyone.
It will all start when they say go.

They are all excited, they're getting in position,
The judge is in place,
Let's start the race.

There is a space race now,
Neil Armstrong is entering,
Hopefully they will see the moon.

'Go!'

Leann Granaghan (11)
St Benedict's RC Primary School

HURRICANE

Bang! There goes the unit on the floor,
And there also goes the car door.
Suddenly there comes off the roof,
I fall over and chip my tooth.
But when the sky is black,
Then it's time for a panic attack.

Tomorrow will be another day,
I hope that I don't fly away.
Gather all your prized possessions
Now it's time for your confessions.
Quickly run, move out of the way,
For now it's nearly judgement day!

Come on, gather up your supplies,
For tomorrow somebody may die.
Hurry up and take cover,
Don't forget your lonely mother,
Look at that weather vane,
For now here's the hurricane.

Oh no! I think I've broke my back,
I hope I don't get a heart attack,
I wonder if my family's well,
I don't know, I cannot tell,
What should I take? I cannot choose,
For I only hear bad news.

Now the hurricane's dying down,
For what I've done, I deserve a crown,
Now I sit down on the tables,
And with my favourite book, Aesop's fables,
At least now, I'm not ill,
And plus the hurricane didn't kill.

Jack Gallagher (11)
St Benedict's RC Primary School

THE DAYDREAM

One little girl,
As quiet as can be
She just sits in the chair,
With her teddy bear.

I wonder what that little girl is thinking of,
When 6am we're in her daydream,
She is riding on a leopard in her
Daydream!

The leopard looks kind of friendly,
I wonder why I am seeing her daydreams
It seems kind of silly,
Is it true?

No don't be silly,
Seeing someone's daydreams
It seems ridiculous,
But can it be?

I can't believe it,
She is daydreaming
She is in the forest, riding a leopard,
Is it because she loves leopards?

Yes this little girl adores leopards,
Her favourite animals is a leopard
I better wake her up now,
Her tea is ready.

Danielle McKenna (9)
St Benedict's RC Primary School

THE SPACE RACE

On your marks, get set, *go!*

The race has begun, NASA vs Martians,
Martians are about to take the lead,
But 'Engines down', they were out.

NASA space shuttle had hit the cruiser,
The space cruiser lit up inside,
'Engines up!' They were back!

The cruiser went into hyperspeed,
The cruiser had took the lead!
NASA turned up the gear,
The command centre gave a cheer.

Neck and neck all the way,
Can NASA save the day?
The finish line is just ahead,
NASA slid into the finish,
I can't believe it, they've just won it.

Curtis McEntee (11)
St Benedict's RC Primary School

THE SPACE RACE

The space race started at nine,
But I didn't have time to dine,
I entered it anyway,
Then started my engine and flew away!

The race was tough but I did my best,
Then I went to Mars and had a rest,
After a while I took off again,
At that moment I saw little green men!

We had a chat for a few minutes,
And then had a game of virtual tennis,
After that I went to the finishing line,
I won and celebrated with a fine cherry wine!

Hitesh Chhaya (9)
St Benedict's RC Primary School

HURRICANE

Out of the wilderness all peaceful and calm,
Where the sea lies,
There was a fortune teller looking at her palm,
Many people die on the seas,
From hurricanes that created through the night.

Rumours spread across the town,
That a hurricane would occur,
So people had their ups and downs,
That thinking the hurricane would come,
So when they saw the weather channel,
They had a sign of relief, for there was no hurricane on the way.

They set out to sea,
To find the trickster who started the rumours,
The winds grew stronger and stronger,
'Tidal wave!' everyone shouted,
Too stupid to move they waited,
Crash! Boom! Slam!
The towners were never heard of again!

Jonathon Christer (11)
St Benedict's RC Primary School

THE TIGER

Padding through the jungle
To go and have a drink
Lapping up the water
Doesn't even blink.

Its sparkly eyes
Its velvety paws
Zebras better watch out
For its snapping jaws.

Its claws are razor sharp
And its tail is swaying back and forth.
Slowly it turns around
And starts heading north.

It looks around its stripes are pointing
Then leaps off into the jungle.

Larrissa Huggard (10)
Sir Frank Whittle Primary School

MY PET DENNIS

I've got a pet ant called Dennis
and he loves playing tennis.
So I played with him
and he looked quite dim.
So I took him to the vet
and I said 'Don't forget,
he's just my little pet.'
So the vet made him well
and now he's looking swell!

Jonathan Pearson (9)
Sir Frank Whittle Primary School

FLOWERS

Flowers blossom in the day
In the special time of May
They are really best in the summer
So we give them to our mother.

All the flowers are colourful and bright
Like a flying coloured kite,
You see them when you walk in the park
And they glitter in the dark.

Sunflowers grow high in the sky
High enough to see the blackbirds fly,
Bees fly in the sky
To suck the pollen so they won't die.

Sufeena Lindsay (9)
Sir Frank Whittle Primary School

CATS

My cat's just had his meningitis jab and
didn't even cry, he was so scared before it
he thought he might die.
Later on that day, at the dinner table his tooth
fell out then he started to cry.
His mother came over and gave him a big kiss.

When he stopped crying he went out to play,
All his friends gathered round admiring the
space in his mouth.

Then it was time to come in and go to bed
zzzzzzzzz

Rosie Langford (10)
Sir Frank Whittle Primary School

FLOWERS

Flowers, flowers
I look for hours
Roses make my nose go funny.

Tulips make my lips go red
And go to my head
I take them and put them by my bed

Poppies are red
And make me feel sloppy
Poppies are purple
And make me go in a circle.

Bluebells are blue
And I like them too.

I love flowers
And pick them for hours.

Lauren Donovan (10)
Sir Frank Whittle Primary School

ART

Art is so great
you don't want to wait.
You make wonderful things
and create fairy wings.
You make what you want
and that's what I call a good
Art lesson!

Kirby Perkin (10)
Sir Frank Whittle Primary School

SNAKES

Slithering anxiously it went through the jungle.
Sneaking across the deadly floor.
Creeping up on its prey
Waiting to go.

Camouflaged amongst the grass
The zigzag creature waits
Spitting like rain.
The zigzag creature waits.

The zigzag creature sprints out
Catching his deadly food.
He soon sits like a bird
As the zigzag creature waits.

Claire Foster (10)
Sir Frank Whittle Primary School

TV

When I went to the BBC
My friends and family wouldn't believe me
I got a question right
And the audience thought I was bright
I got one wrong and had to pass
Suddenly I hit the jackpot, I won the cash!

I went on soaps too
And things popstars like to do.
I was famous really
I love my life dearly
But being famous is not my style at all
But most people still think I'm cool!

Laura Barrett (9)
Sir Frank Whittle Primary School

TIN MONSTER

There was a monster who lived in a bin
who was entirely made from tin.
The monster went to a disco bar
and drove away in a Jaguar car.
When he went to bed he dreamt he was king
and he started to sing.
When he woke up in his bed
he said he had only once piece of bread.
Then he went in a can
And got shipped off to Japan.
When he came back he got a smack
from his mum who ate humans called Mack.
He also got grounded by his mum
whose head went really quite numb.
'Cause of the things tin monster did,
by the way, tin monster's name is Sid.

Adam Brown (9)
Sir Frank Whittle Primary School

EAGLE

The golden eagle
Its eyes like fireballs glowing.

It swoops, it glides
It pounces like a spring.

It grabs its prey with its razor-sharp claws.
Sharp as pins and needles.

Its eyes stare at you
With a ferocious look.

Wayne Cole (11)
Sir Frank Whittle Primary School

FOOTBALL WITH MAN U

Football's coming home
with a goal
To win the match, it's coming
Football's coming home

With all the goals we would score
We wouldn't lose
With Beckham and Moore

Don't mess with us
Because you won't beat us
Because we are the best
With all Man U

With Giggs getting his hat-trick
To win the game
Make Man U still the best

Football's coming home
3 - 0 Victory

Craig Hands (10)
Sir Frank Whittle Primary School

FRIENDSHIP

I have a friend, she's really nice,
Her name is Keeley Wilson.
We always stick together,
She always sticks up for me
And I always stick up for her.
There was a bully in our school
But me and my mate, we stick together.

Danielle Simone Dutton (10)
Sir Frank Whittle Primary School

SCHOOL

I like school because
It's very cool
although I ought to learn
Much more, because I don't
even know what four and four is.
Do you?

But when it's playtime
I run around
Sometimes I find a pound,
but I can't believe my eyes,
So I fall to the ground.

Then all my friends are crowding round
then there is a sound in the air
I look up and there is a
Teddy bear.

Abbie Griffiths (9)
Sir Frank Whittle Primary School

MY FRIEND'S CAT

My friend's cat
is covered in black.
He won't stay still,
he's always on the move.

His name
is Fame.
When he says 'Yes'
he wiggles his tail.

He hides upstairs
and then jumps out.
He tries to kill bumbles,
he only has to use his knees.

You don't have to shout,
you only have to whisper.
He listens to you first thing.

Sarah Conlon (10)
Sir Frank Whittle Primary School

HAVE YOU SEEN A PIG FLY?

One frosty morning,
When cloudy was the weather.
I saw a huge pig fly,
As light as a feather.

The pig was huge,
It was fat and pink.
And one last thing,
It really did stink!

It had huge white wings,
As white as milk.
Its body looked smooth,
As smooth as silk.

It made a snort,
As loud as a bear.
It started to go faster,
Heading for the fair!

Rebecca Claire Phythian (10)
Sir Frank Whittle Primary School

THE SPACE RACE!

Up, up high
A spaceship in the sky.
The alien was weird
He had a long beard
The spaceships would be there,
Flying in the air.

On your marks, get set, go
Gosh don't they go slow?
Only a few are fast,
They won't come last.
One has crashed,
And someone has just passed.

Who wins the race
That happened in
Space?

Lucy Ridding (9)
Sir Frank Whittle Primary School

LOVE ME

Love is all around us,
Love is in the air.
Love will stay with us,
Love will never end.
Love is always good,
Love is sometimes sad.
But there is something about love.
There is nothing as good as love.

Karl Gemmell (10)
Sir Frank Whittle Primary School

SWEET ICE CREAM

Ice cream, ice cream is the best
Vanilla, chocolate and the rest,
Strawberry, mint, raspberry ripple
That's enough to make me dribble

Strawberry sauce and chocolate flakes
It's so much better than fairy cakes
Ice lollies, ice lollies, yum yum yum
If you don't like them, you're really dumb.

Mint chocolate chip, cookies and cream
Yum, yum, yum that's all I need
Blackcurrant lollies, orange too
Ice cream, ice cream I love you!

Vanisha Mistry (9)
Sir Frank Whittle Primary School

RAKI THE RAT

Raki loves sausages, beans and chips,
He likes playing in my toy ships,
He doesn't like school,
but Raki's cool!

He chills out with Sass,
she's a nice lass,
I don't like her much,
but boys think she's a nice touch.

He doesn't like peas.
He sails over seas.
Snow he just loves.
He's friends with two white doves.

Jade Bagshaw (9)
Sir Frank Whittle Primary School

CHILDREN ON THE PLAYGROUND

Children on the playground having lots of fun,
Keeping safe by watching where they're going.
You should be careful if you're going to run.
Being kind, playing, what fun they're having.
Staying close by to their friends and things,
When the bell rings be sure to stay still.
In an assembly be sure to really sing,
This is the way that is sure to make you ill.
Children on the playground, staying in a crowd,
Having lots of fun is sure to make you proud.
The is the way that children on the playground play.

Charlotte McDonnell (10)
Sir Frank Whittle Primary School

TIGER

Roaming and sneaking through the jungle,
looking for prey.
Suddenly it spots a wild boar.
Flattening his pointy, black ears,
It's stalking the prey with its
emerald green eyes.
It sneaks, still crouched down,
as quiet as a mouse.
Still the wild boar suspects nothing.
A large pounce, a squeal.
The tiger has caught its prey.
Roaring the hyenas away
while it carries its prey into the deep jungle.
It rips it up in private.

Eleanor Joanne Smith (10)
Sir Frank Whittle Primary School

Fox

Crafty as a dog
Sly as a fox
Snapping through the trees
Quiet as a mouse
Fast as a cheetah
Smells like my gym socks.

Among the trees
Across the landscape
Drinks like a whale
Eats like a pig
Big bushy tail just like a bush
It preys like a hawk.

Watching its prey run.
Its big red eyes glaring straight at you.

Carl Gardner (11)
Sir Frank Whittle Primary School

SNOW

I looked out my window this morning,
the ground was full of snow.
All the squirrels that lived in the woods,
rightly decided to go.

They have hidden all their nuts away,
as they are sure to come back
on a brighter day.

Llewelyn Venter (10)
Sir Frank Whittle Primary School

HARRY POTTER

Harry Potter, the wizard
Lives with the Muggles.

His auntie and uncle
He hates them and Dudley too.

Ron and Hermione
His best friends, they are wizards too.

Hogwarts is the best school
With broomsticks, frogs and self-shuffling snap.

He's been in a lot of mischief with the trolls
and you know who.

He's got glasses
with a nasty lightning scar.

He's always trying his best
but not always getting there!

Zoe Allsopp (10)
Sir Frank Whittle Primary School

GORILLAS

Swinging tree to tree
Travelling in troops
Sleeping in the canopy.

The gang leader
Bigger than anyone else
Leads them into danger
Shows them how to hunt.

Michael Maddy (10)
Sir Frank Whittle Primary School

LION

Sneaking through the long, spiky grass,
Quiet as a tiger.
With golden coloured fur,
He can't say anything
So he can't shout 'Sir.'

The lions are fast and they catch food,
When they can't catch food they go in a mood.
On their fur are ants,
They don't look anything like plants.

They have gritting teeth.
They are very muscley.
When they are in the tree,
They catch a flee.
They have brown eyes
On their fur they have flies.

Maisie Regan (10)
Sir Frank Whittle Primary School

THE ALIEN SPACECRAFT

In the strange place it is as round as a cylinder
And as colourful as the rainbow.

The explosive devices *boom* like a double barrelled shotgun!
The alien's antennas vibrate like a PlayStation's controller.

He sounds like a TV when it goes wrong
He floats like a cloud, he plays on the computer like a
                                  complicated puzzle.

His mind is as sharp as a pin
And he is as busy as a bee.

Saba Ali (8)
Walsgrave CE Primary School

THE ALIEN SPACECRAFT!

The computers are as wobbly as jelly on a plate,
when the spacecraft lands on Earth,
spacecraft celebrates the birth.

An alien floating around,
sleeping on computers all day and night,
sleeping as quiet as a little mouse.

She's green and wears a little pink bow.

She's always jumping on Earth
as quick as lightning.
Eyes as big as bowling balls
people taking them out to play.
They are as fat as Santa Claus.
She's as colourful as a rainbow.

Phillipa Lea (8)
Walsgrave CE Primary School

TASTE

I like the taste of

Some salty chips crunching in my mouth,
A prickly pineapple prickling on my tastebuds.

I like the taste of

A handful of sugary sweets rotting in my mouth,
Hot lemony pancakes tickling my tastebuds.

I like the taste of

Some saucy spaghetti wriggling in my mouth,
Some creamy chocolate melting on my tastebuds.

I like the taste of

Chunky cheese all chewy in my mouth,
Some hot doughnuts treating my tastebuds.

Jeenal Parekh (11)
Walsgrave CE Primary School

THE ALIEN SPACECRAFT

Buttons flash like a thousand stars,
knobs glitter and twinkle like the end of a rainbow,
the wires are like snakes and gunge hangs off the ceiling.
Peering through buttons is a jelly alien,
dashing off like lightning through the door.
He is as weird as an 18 legged octopus,
as he sneezes his ears pop out like an African elephant.
He leaves a slimy trail of gunge behind him like a snail.
His voice sounds like a car speeding,
the alien is working on the complicated computer,
looking for other planets and other things on the planets.
He has 18 eyes, 10 ears and mouths,
his eyes are the size of footballs,
his ears are very weird
and he talks really strangely,
making you feel like you are an alien too . . .

Chelsea Buckley (7)
Walsgrave CE Primary School

AMBLE OR SCRAMBLE

Ducks waddle
Pups paddle

Flies zap
Birds flap

Rabbits eat
Deer leap

Geese follow
Hippos wallow

Mice hide
Seagulls glide

Elephants amble
Monkeys scramble

Elephants stamp -
But -

I stomp!

Sabastion Jefferies (9)
Walsgrave CE Primary School

TOUCH

Touching all day long,
Holding my ice-cold milk,
Squashing a rubber ball.

Touching all day long,
Throwing and catching hard balls,
Putting my soft rabbit into its den.

Touching all day long,
Picking sticky glue off my fingers,
Putting a wet flannel on my face.

Touching all day long,
Getting conkers out of their prickly case,
Holding the PlayStation control when vibrating.

Lawrence Vinicombe (11)
Walsgrave CE Primary School

WIGGLE AND GIGGLE

Flamingos waddle
Ducks paddle

Tigers pride
Cheetahs hide

Lions growl
Wolves howl

Pups bounce
Cats pounce

Bulls charge
Monkeys barge

Kangaroos hop
Horses clop

Worms wiggle -
But -
I *giggle!*

Charlotte Faulkner (7)
Walsgrave CE Primary School

BABE PIG IN THE CITY

B abe is a pig
A very pink pig
B right as a button
E asily a glutton

P ig in the city saves his friends
I n a family of monkeys he depends
G rowling dogs chasing round lots of bends

I nto the water the dog goes
N ipping and biting at Babe's toes

T hrough the water goes the dog
H earing the fearful hog
E veryone laughing because on his nose is a sock

C ome Babe to the rescue
I hear you are great
T o the dog you go
Y ou can do it Babe, I think so!

Ellie Reynolds (7)
Walsgrave CE Primary School

JUST LOOK AT WHAT HAPPENS AT CHRISTMAS

Family comes round
making a sound
of their feet on the ground.

Lots of girls
with their hair in curls
are eating chocolate swirls.

Too many sweets in their chests
so they should have a rest
because they don't feel at their best.

The presents under the tree
make the children dance with glee
just like me.

Tiffany Roberts (11)
Walsgrave CE Primary School

MUNCH OR CRUNCH

Kangaroos bounce
Puppies pounce

Lions stride
Seagulls glide

Elephants amble
Chickens scramble

Horses clop
Cats hop

Rabbits munch
Bears crunch

Worms wriggle
Dogs jiggle

Bees zip -
But -
I skip!

Abigail Jackson (7)
Walsgrave CE Primary School

ZOOM AND BOOM

Flies zip
Bees flip

Cheetahs zoom
Elephants boom

Tigers bounce
Lions pounce

Mice hurry
Hamsters scurry

Bears fuzz
Bees buzz

Cats race
Dogs chase

Parrots talk -
But -
I *walk!*

Charis Moreland (9)
Walsgrave CE Primary School

TASTE

I like the taste of
A juicy orange slipping in my mouth
Salty crisps make my tastebuds tingle.

I like the taste of
A yummy tomato so juicy in my mouth
Lots of crunchy cucumber in my mouth.

I like the taste of
Sugary sweets make my teeth rot
A prickly pineapple makes my tastebuds pop.

I like the taste of
Chunky cheese chewy in my mouth
A crunchy carrot making my tastebuds tingle.

Matthew Hunt (10)
Walsgrave CE Primary School

AMBLE OR SCRAMBLE

Cats race
Tigers chase

Mice scurry
Birds hurry

Giraffes stride
Seagulls glide

Horses clop
Rabbits hop

Flies zip
Bees flip

Elephants amble
Chickens scramble

Bulls charge -
But -
I *barge!*

Naomi Patel (8)
Walsgrave CE Primary School

ZAP AND SNAP

Horses gallop
Hippos wallop

Elephants amble
Parrots scramble

Swallows glide
Lions stride

Turtles trot
Donkeys clop

Hares jump
Camels hump

Cheetahs zap
Crocodiles snap

Flies zip -
But -
I *skip.*

Ian Rhodes (7)
Walsgrave CE Primary School

TOUCH

I do not like the feel of
Cold, slimy, sticky tar,
Or runny glue sticking my fingers together.
I do not like the feel of
A scratchy duvet after it's been washed,
Or prickly thorns on a rose bush.

I like the feel of
A tickly towel, after it's come off the radiator,
And freezing ice melting in my fingers.
I like the feel of
My rabbit's warm and soft fur against my cheek,
And soft snow dripping through my hands.

Laura Marriott (10)
Walsgrave CE Primary School

CANTER OR FANTA

Kangaroos bounce
Kittens pounce

Worms wiggle
Bugs jiggle

Dogs race
Lions chase

Mice hide
Snakes slide

Tigers attack
Bees zap

Elephants boom
Cheetahs zoom

Horses canter
But -
I drink Fanta!

Courtney Weaver-Ennis (8)
Walsgrave CE Primary School

THE ALIEN SPACECRAFT

Buttons flash like a thousand stars,
knobs glitter and twinkle
like the end of the rainbow.
The wires are like
snakes and gunge hangs off the solid ceiling.
Peering through the buttons is an alien as colourful as a jelly.
Dashes of lightning through the creaking door.
He is as weird as an 18 legged octopus
as he sneezes his big elephant ears come out.
He leaves behind
a slimy gunge all over the place.
He is trying to get to a peaceful planet.
He speaks to an old creaking door
to other aliens to get home.
The button covers the whole of the computer
like a computerised puzzle.

Kirstie Smith (7)
Walsgrave CE Primary School

WHAT'S IT LIKE TO BE A BEE

I have been scary for too long.
I have seen too many people run from me.

You think you're the only one that suffers from the things that I can do,
But I suffer too, because once I have stung you, I . . . die.

I look like a sleeping policeman on the road,
With my beautiful see-through wings like crystals in the sun.

I live in a hive on an oak tree in the wood,
You don't know it but you need me.

I make you honey and then you take it and leave me
No reward, not even a thank you.

I want to be treated as a friend
Not an enemy.

Camille-Louise McCullagh (11)
Walsgrave CE Primary School

SIGHT

I like to see . . .
Bright coloured fireworks exploding in the dark night-time sky,
A layer of crisp brown leaves all over the floor.

I like to see . . .
Fat, brown ducks swimming on a pond,
Cool, blue rippling water.

I like to see . . .
Bouncy white clouds drifting by,
Bright flowers, an explosion of colour.

I like to see . . .
A starry night, like a black piece of paper, covered in sequins,
Trees in winter, sparkling with frost.

I like to see . . .
The crisp twinkle of a snow-covered floor,
The bright colours of a rainbow on a dull, grey background.

Lucy Glasscoe (10)
Walsgrave CE Primary School

DEEP IN THE JUNGLE

Deep in the jungle, scary, scary jungle
along came a monkey screaming like a banshee;
through the trees of the jungle
along came a Siberian tiger
staring at his prey
deep, deep, the sound of the jungle
deep, deep, the sound of the jungle
along came a snake
slithering through the lake
along came an elephant
stampeding through the jungle
with a mighty thump
then there was silence
only to be broken by a mighty roar.

Jordan Sargent (9)
Walsgrave CE Primary School

WIGGLE OR JIGGLE

Lions prowl
Wolves howl

Giraffe stride
Mice hide

Pups pounce
Cats bounce

Bulls charge
Monkeys barge

Flamingos waddle
Ducks paddle

Stingrays swim -
But -
I *win!*

Cameron Dhesi (7)
Walsgrave CE Primary School

THE ALIEN SPACECRAFT

It's as colourful as a rainbow.
As round as the earth.
It's as big as England.
It has hundreds of windows like a hospital.

Hundreds of computers like a computer factory.
In the computer room there is a creature stomping
Around like a herd of elephants.

His eyes glowing in the darkness like two gleaming torches.
The gunge coming from his mouth is as runny as lava.

His slobber is as red as blood.
As he stomps he wobbles like jelly.
His looking eyes are as sharp as pins.

He senses an intruder.
He stomps like an elephant looking for me.
'*Oh no!*' He's spotted me. He's licking his lips
Like an animal that's spotted its prey.

Toni-Marie Jackson (8)
Walsgrave CE Primary School

STRIDE OR GLIDE

Werewolves howl
Tigers growl

        Giraffes stride
        Seagulls glide

Kangaroos bounce
Kittens pounce

        Horses clop
        Rabbits hop

Lions roar
Parrots soar

        Cats race
        Dogs chase

Tigers talk
But -
I walk!

Awais Ali (7)
Walsgrave CE Primary School

SPIDER

People have always been terrified of me,
Some even think I am evil.
But I am so small,
I have done nothing wrong.
Children torture me,
They pull my legs off one by one.
Some even stamp on my friends and kill them.

I am small, dark and hairy,
I have 8 little legs,
I try to be nice,
Like cleaning their baths,
But people still reject me.

Will they ever like me?

Lucy Howe (10)
Walsgrave CE Primary School

WIGGLE OR GIGGLE

Flamingos waddle
Ducks paddle

Tigers pride
Cheetahs hide

Lions growl
Lynx howl

Pups pounce
Cats bounce

Bulls charge
Monkeys barge

Kangaroos hop
Horses clop

Parrots talk -
But -
I *walk!*

Hannah Tyler (7)
Walsgrave CE Primary School

SWIMMING AND WINNING

Dinosaurs roar
Larks soar

Frogs jump
Bulls bump

Giraffes stride
Kittens hide

Bees buzz
Bears fuzz

Flies zoom
Elephants boom

Cats chase
Mice race

Tortoise swim
But -
I win!

Connor Robinson (8)
Walsgrave CE Primary School

TOUCH

Touch my freezing Antarctic milk
Feel my soft duvet,
Touch the breeze on a wrinkly tree
And the feel of a prickly hairband.

You're touching every day and night.

Touch the *massive* conker shell
Very spiky and round,
Feel my hard plastic chair
And my vibration on my PlayStation control.

You're touching every day and night.

Sean Kenney (10)
Walsgrave CE Primary School

SOAR OR ROAR

Seagulls soar,
Lions roar.

Bugs scuttle,
Seals huddle.

Bees flit,
Fleas nip.

Larks swoop,
Cheetahs zoom.

Parrots perch,
Cats search.

Tigers growl,
Wolves howl.

Dogs walk,
But I *talk!*

Mark Stringer (8)
Walsgrave CE Primary School

ANIMALS

The dog is chasing the rabbit,
running like the wind.

The cat is having a nap,
like a ball of wool.

The eagle is in its nest,
like a mouse in its hole.

The mole is digging,
like rolling a ball.

The cow is mooing,
like the sound of the rain.

The mouse is jumping,
like a wild wind.

The cat is hissing,
like the thunder.

The cheetah is running
like Thrust 3.

Charlotte Gibbons (11)
Walsgrave CE Primary School

JAMAICA

Jamaica, I think of sea and sand,
It's a very beautiful land,
And on the sand,
There's always a reggae band!

The climate, it is very hot,
Outside, around a baking pot,
It is always very hot,
Except at night when it's not!

The sea is clear,
They drink lots of beer,
Their water is clear,
The music is nice to hear!

Aarron Macauley (10)
Walsgrave CE Primary School

ANIMAL ACTIVITIES

The dog is chasing the rabbit,
Running like the wind.
While the cat is having a nap,
Curled up like a ball of wool.

The bat is flying around a tree,
Like a bird looking for food.
While the owl hunts for a home,
Like a sparrow looking for a mate.

A tiger prowls around his land,
Like a spy creeping around.
While an elephant is sleeping
Like a log on the floor.

The monkey is eating his food,
Like he has not eaten for months.
While a kingfisher is diving in a pond,
Like a diver in the Olympics.

The ant is scurrying around on the floor,
Like a person running from a volcano.
While a pig is gobbling his food,
Like a very hungry person.

Erika Shuttleworth (10)
Walsgrave CE Primary School

THE ALIEN SPACECRAFT

The room is as round as a fat juicy orange,
and the windows look
like a jewelled headband looking
straight at me.
The spacecraft is as green
as a blade of grass.
The gadgets are moved
as fast as a cheetah.
The alien is so fat
he's stuck to 12 chairs like glue,
he has 34 tentacles
that stick up like Scooby Doo's ears,
when he hears the word food.
He has twelve heads as big as dragon's eggs.
24 legs like the roots of a tree.
24 arms like streamers.
The alien's voice is like a creaking door.
The alien is working at the computer so fast
like he is as mad as a hatter.
He senses an intruder
but he cannot find me
as I am camouflaged
as a man in the army.

Sarah Earle (8)
Walsgrave CE Primary School

THE WITCH'S KITCHEN

In the witch's kitchen there is:

1 big black cooking pot
Covered in yellow spots.

2 fat frogs
Sitting on logs.

3 slithering newts with
24 shiny boots.

4 spiders crawling
Across the floor, look!

5 more crawling up the door.

6 furry mice playing
With dice.

7 scary snakes
Fresh from the lakes.

8 ghosts from hell
With a terrible smell.

9 bees eating fleas
In small trees, and

10 hens in a big pen
Which is their den.

Georgia Jay Downie (9)
Walsgrave CE Primary School